50 Things To Help You Win

In Life, Money and Relationships

Developed By Sharon D. Fiberesima
For Scribal Publishing

Contributors: Adenike Olasimbo
Angela Ohiorenoya. Emmanuel Olatokun
Ginikachukwu John Ibeagha
Joseph Omeiza. Michael Isichei
Ngozi Ketochi-Ekpo. Orifie Uyo
Otonye Inwang. Seun Omoha
Sunmbo Lizzy Olatunji
Sharon D. Fiberesima

Scribal

Scribal Publishing
London

Copyright

Copyright © 2025 by Sharon D. Fiberesima
The right of Scribal Publishing to be identified as the author of this work has been asserted by the author in accordance with the Copyright, Designs and Patents Act 1988

ISBN: 978-1-06-834505-0

All rights reserved. Except for brief excerpts for review purposes, no part of this book may be reproduced or used in any form without written permission from the publisher.

Scripture taken from the New King James Version®. Copyright © 1982 by Thomas Nelson. Used by permission. All rights reserved.

Scripture quotations marked (NIV) are taken from the Holy Bible, New International Version®, NIV®. Copyright © 1973, 1978, 1984, 2011 by Biblica, Inc.™ Used by permission of Zondervan. All rights reserved worldwide. www.zondervan.com The "NIV" and "New International Version" are trademarks registered in the United States Patent and Trademark Office by Biblica, Inc.™

50 Things To Help You Win: In Life, Money and Relationships

First published in 2025 by Scribal Publishing, London
www.JustScribal.co.uk

Contributors

Adenike Olasimbo
Adenike is a Practice Nurse and the founder of *Tiffany Events*. She also serves as the Events Lead and Dance Coordinator for youngsters in her church. Married to Dr Tomiwa Olasimbo, she is a proud mother of three lovely daughters—Harmony, Tiffany, and Destiny.

Adenike is passionate about helping the younger generation maximise their full potential and believes that excellence is not limited to a single pursuit. She hopes her words encourage others to embrace every gift within them and live purposefully in all they do.

Angela Ohiorenoya
Angela is a singer, song writer and one of the worship leaders in Victory Assembly, Sheffield.
She has a passion to lead people into Spirit-led and spirit-filled worship. One that is honest and sincere. She's written and released songs that have been a blessing to people all over the globe.

She has ministered in conferences, prayer gatherings and churches across Europe and Africa, including Festival of Life UK, and several other worship events.

Angela is a teacher by profession from Sheffield Hallam University. She's currently studying.

She's married and blessed with two lovely children.

Emmanuel Olatokun
Emmanuel Olatokun (PhD) more commonly known as DrE is a Kingdom ambassador and teacher of the word. He has an unquenchable desire to see people reach their God given potential by fully manifesting purpose to the fullest. DrE loves to build and develop people through the gift of teaching, public speaking, mentoring, coaching and training.

With an doctorate degree in Knowledge Management and years of experience as a Business/Functional Consultant, DrE likes to challenge and confront conventional thinking and stereotypical philosophies with the aim to reset mental paradigm. DrE is also a career coach and a intrapreneur. He is married to his wife Bukky and they have 2 lovely girls.

Ginikachukwu John Ibeagha
Ginikachukwu is an accomplished Nigerian professional and entrepreneur, currently based in Almere, Netherlands, who is deeply committed to his family, faith, and ventures outside of the corporate world. As a dedicated husband and father of two children, he balances his professional achievements with personal passions, finding enjoyment in playing football, travelling, and focusing on understanding the ways of God.

His entrepreneurial drive is evident as the co-founder, alongside his wife, of **The Jollof Place** (www.thejollofplace.nl), a food service establishment centred on African cuisine which has achieved year-on-year growth since its founding in 2020.

Professionally, he is a seasoned Manager, Solutions Architect, and Pre-Sales Leader with over 13 years of experience. He is recognised in his field as a skilled public speaker and mentor.

Joseph Omeiza

Joseph is a Director at Broadview Management Services, a UK-based management consultancy. He holds a Bachelor's degree in Electronics and Communications Engineering from the University of Sheffield, as well as two Master's degrees: one in Engineering with Business Management from King's College London and another in Tourism Management from Sheffield Business School.

A passionate advocate for personal finance, investment, and wealth creation, Joseph believes that anyone can build lasting financial security through knowledge, discipline, and intentional action.

Michael Isichei

Dr. Michael Isichei is an award-winning educator, consultant, entrepreneur and academic and professional coach dedicated to empowering students and professionals through expert guidance in communication, research, and global mobility. With a passion for lifelong learning and a commitment to excellence, he has helped thousands navigate academic and career challenges, equipping them with the skills and confidence to succeed.

Ngozi Ketochi-Ekpo

Pastor (Mrs) Ngozi Ketochi-Ekpo who is fondly called Mrs Pkay is a Personable multifaceted individual who is passionate about taking care of God's people and has made significant contributions in the different ways that has found expression.

A Life Coach, she has a burning passion to nurture single ladies and help them maximize their single season intentionally.

She is the author of *Why Am I Here*? A very relatable and reflective book that equips young individuals, Visionaries and Pioneers to navigate tough seasons in their journey to manifesting.

She is also the CEO of Xristekay Ventures, a food and catering company with subsidiaries Xristies cakes, Xristies Pot and Naijaclaypotchef.

Beyond her successful business and Career, Mrs Ngozi Ketochi is recognised for her ministry gifts, as she is passionate about pushing God's kingdom agenda.

She is also an ardent humanitarian who focuses on women, children and the less privileged. She spends most of her time, resources and intellect giving back to people around her and the society at large.

She is the Pioneer of the *Marriage Bound Gems* initiative for young ladies, an NGO responsible for raising single ladies and helping them maximise their single season. She has successfully created this community to foster spiritual growth, professional development and personal growth for these young ladies.

She, alongside her husband Pastor Ketochi-Ekpo gave life to *The Fruitful Place,* a temporary home and safe place for singles in their transitioning phase of life.

Orifie Uyo
Orifie Uyo is a Human Potential Optimization Expert and "People Builder" committed to identifying and intentionally developing the inherent potential in individuals and organisations to achieve measurable results. An alumna of the University of Ibadan, London School of Economics and Political Science with degrees in Law, Business Consultancy, Public Policy, Arden University, and Montessori Education (adolescents 12–18), she began her career in litigation and commercial law before joining Nigeria LNG Limited (NLNG), where she has held senior advisory roles in strategic corporate stakeholder relations.

A Certified Executive Coach, she specialises in strengths, performance and results coaching, organisational culture, and career analysis,

Orifie helps mid- to senior-level professional women design optimal professional and personal lives. She created MESchool—a self-discovery and life-strategy seminar delivered across Africa, North America, and Europe. An ardent believer in adolescent development, she founded Nigeria's first Adolescent Montessori school in 2022 - Archersfield Montessori Academy - to cultivate the knowledge, practical skills, and confidence young people need to thrive.

Bringing together legal, business, policy, and educational perspectives with a deep understanding of human behaviour and organisational dynamics, Orifie is known for strategic vision, innovative thinking, and deft navigation of complex challenges in the management of issues, reputation, sustainability, organisational culture, and non-technical risks.

She served for over five years on the executive of the NLNG Women's Initiative Network (NWIN), earning recognition for meritorious service and advancing gender equity. She also founded and sits on the board of a coaching and mentoring programme for young people aged 13–30.

An author of over 40 books, she is a member of the Nigerian Bar Association (NBA), International Association of Business Communicators (IABC), Nigerian Institute of Public Relations (NIPR), and Association Montessori Internationale (AMI), as well as The

Room and The Eagles' Nest Mastermind; she also serves on the Harvard Business Review Advisory Council.

Otonye Inwang
A strategic HR professional and aspiring consultant, Otonye Inwang has spent nearly a decade solving people-related challenges across diverse industries, from consulting and finance to e-commerce and non-profits. Passionate about behavioral science, the human potential, and the future of work, she dedicated to unlocking productivity and performance through innovative, people-centric solutions.

Seun Omoha
Seun is the author of the Her Father's Daughter books and the founder of Being Super Woman (BSW)—an initiative created to equip and empower professional Christian women in the marketplace. She is married to Silas Omoha, and together they reside in the United Kingdom with their daughter.

Sunmbo Lizzy Olatunji
Olasunmbo is a devoted mother of three—Oluwasetemipe, Oluwadamire, and Oluwafirekun Olatunji. She is deeply passionate about instilling lasting values, morals, and cultural heritage in the next generation. Through her words and actions, Lizzy seeks to preserve meaningful legacies and inspire others to do the same. She hopes her contribution to this volume serves as a gentle guide and reminder of the importance of passing on what truly matters.

Sharon D. Fiberesima
Sharon is a writer, editor, and creative coach passionate about helping others bring their God-given ideas to life through words. With over fifteen years of experience in writing and publishing, she leads Scribal Publishing, a faith-inspired company dedicated to excellence in storytelling and purposeful communication.

Her work blends creativity, faith, and a deep desire to see lives transformed through the written word. Sharon believes that stories and values—when shared intentionally—have the power to shape generations.

Dedication

For:

Alicia,
Ehi,
Aliyah-Victoria and Erin,
Kendrick and Audrey,
Natasha and Nathan,
Thea, Abiye, Dein and Talia,
Zoe and Jemima,
Destiny, Harmony and Tiffany,
Uche and Adaeze,
Oluwasetemipe, Oluwadamire and Oluwafirekunm,
Kokoette, Otonye, Etete, Jennifer, Bridget and Mayen,

XIV

Acknowledgements

Special thanks to God, the Father of all creation, for His help, guidance, and steady hand throughout this project.

My heartfelt appreciation goes to every contributor — this book would not exist without your voices and your generosity.

To *Hephzibah Anosike*, our gifted editor, thank you for the excellence, insight, and care you brought to this work.

And finally, to everyone who reads or picks up this book: thank you. This book was written with you in mind, and I pray it blesses you deeply.

Table of Contents

50 Things To Help You Win III
   Copyright IV
   Contributors V
   Dedication XIII
   Acknowledgements XV
   Table of Contents XVII
   Introduction XXI
   How to Use This Book XXV
50 Things To Help You Win XXVII

Part One: Know Yourself, The Foundation of Everything 9
   Shaping Your Life Through Your Thoughts 13
   You are Exactly Who You Were Meant to Be 17
   You Are So Loved 21
   Own and Believe in Your Voice 23
   You Are Strong, You Are Bold, You Are Brave 27
   Shine Anyway 31
   Growth is a Process 35
   Seek Transformation Above Popularity 39
   Your Biggest Job in Life is to Understand Yourself 41
   Mastering Your Emotions 45

Part Two: Money Matters, Understanding Finance Early 49
   Learn about Money as Early as Possible 51
   Solve Problems, Create Value 53
   Save and Invest: Money is a Seed 55
   Be Generous: Look for Ways to Give 57
   Be Content with What You Have Now 59

Value the Labour of Others 61
Stewardship: Avoid Debt and Use Money Wisely 63
Entrepreneurship: Start Small, Think Big............. 65

Part Three: People & Relationships – Building Connections That Last... 69
Never Beg for Love or Acceptance 71
Respect Everyone 73
Respect Yourself.. 75
Choose Your Friends Carefully 77
Forgive Quickly and Fully...................................... 81
Conflict Resolution: Learn to Talk It Out............... 83
Digital Friendships and Social Media Boundaries .. 85
Have Trusted Advisors.. 87

Part Four: Growing in Self-Worth and Resilience....... 91
Confidence Comes from Doing, Not Just Knowing.. 95
Hard Work and the Extra Mile 97
Seek Excellence... 99
Integrity, Honesty, and Character Matter............. 103
It's OK To Make Mistakes 107
Life's Twists and Turns: Stay Flexible 109
There Is Always a Way Out 111
Decide to Decide Well 113
Practice Diligence 115
Be Restless... 117
Flip the Switch: Choosing Gratitude 119
Listen More 121

Part Five: Living with Purpose and Pursuing Excellence 125

Learn How You *Learn* and Never Be Afraid to Aim High 129

Follow Your Interests 133

See Before You *See*... 137

The Dreams You Conceive Now Can Be Your Future 139

Everyone's Journey Is Different 141

Run Your Own Race.. 145

Opportunities Lead to Opportunities 147

Make Hay While the Sun Shines 151

Part Six: Anchored in God 155

Put God First 157

Anchored in God 161

I Can Do All Things Through Christ Who Strengthens Me 165

You Are a Leader – And Leadership Starts with You 167

Bonus Lessons: Treasures for the Journey 171

What to Do When You're Tempted 175

Watch What They Do 177

Your Getting Starts from Giving 179

The Power of Recognition: Learning to Notice Difference 183

Respect Time: Use It Wisely................................ 187

Conclusion.. 189

xx

Foreword

Wining in life is a wonderful thing. To win means to have successful results in your endeavours, to overcome obstacles and challenges you encounter along the way of your dream, and to successfully accomplish your goals. The opposite of winning is losing, suffering defeat, failing, and the inability to have your best results. Everyone likes to win and no one likes to lose.

It is possible to win consistently and in all aspects of life when God is in the equation. This is because the Bible says in 2 Corinthians 2:14 that God will cause us to triumph in Christ, in every place. Therefore, you can win in your relationships, you can win in your career aspirations. You can win with money, achieve your dream future and become all that you set your mind on becoming.

This is what this book is all about and I wholeheartedly recommend it to you and everyone you would love to see have and enjoy a wonderful and fulfilling life.

'50 Things to Help You Win: In Life, Money & Relationships' is well thought through and written; it is coming out of the life and many years of experiences of the authors who carefully put the book together.

In this book you will learn how the right attitude or mind-set can transform you into a winner. You will learn how to turn defeat to success, to navigate through life's challenges and obstacles; and how to be in control and succeed.

This is written to help the reader in making the best life choices and to power them on the journey to their best life.

Study it methodically. Get a copy for a friend and share with your family.

Happy reading everyone.

Pastor Musa Bako
RCCG Victory Assembly
Sheffield

Introduction

Why These 50 Lessons Matter

Every generation faces its own battles: new technologies, new opportunities, new pressures, new stressors. Yet, beneath it all, the questions remain the same: *Who am I? What matters most? How do I live well?*

This book was born from those questions. It is a collection of simple truths, timeless values, and practical wisdom gathered over years of learning, reflection, and faith. These lessons are not theories from a classroom, but real-life insights—tested through experience, shaped by mistakes, strengthened by grace, and inspired by the hope that young hearts can be guided before the world becomes too noisy to listen.

The world today celebrates speed, appearance, and achievement. But real success runs deeper. It begins inside—with character, purpose, and an understanding of who you are in God. That's why these fifty lessons matter. They are not about being perfect; they are about growing strong, thinking deeply, and living wisely. They teach you how to make decisions with integrity, manage money with wisdom, build relationships with respect, and stand tall in a world that sometimes tries to make you small.

Each lesson is short enough to read in minutes but powerful enough to shape a lifetime. Think of them as gentle conversations—evergreen truths shine like a lamp, guiding your steps through the hazy paths of life.

Don't just read these pages. I invite you to take your time. Reflect. Discuss. Question. Practise. The goal isn't to rush through the book—it's to let the book grow through you.

If you live even a handful of these lessons, you'll discover what many people spend years searching for: a life rooted in purpose, guided by wisdom, and anchored in love.

Sharon D. Fiberesima

How to Use This Book

This book isn't meant to be read in one sitting and forgotten, it's designed to be lived with. Each of the 50 lessons (plus bonus lessons) is a seed of wisdom that can grow into real change when you pause, reflect, and apply it to your daily life.

Here are a few ways to get the most from it:

1. Read slowly, think deeply.
Each lesson is short but rich. Read one at a time, maybe one lesson a day or a week and give yourself space to think about it. Ask, "How does this apply to me right now?"

2. Reflect and write.
Keep a notebook or journal nearby. Jot down what stands out to you, how the lesson connects with your experiences, and what actions you can take. Writing helps wisdom stick.

3. Discuss and share.
These lessons are even more powerful when shared. Talk about them with friends, family, or mentors. Use them as conversation starters, devotionals, or study prompts.

4. Revisit often.
As you grow, you'll see new meanings in old lessons. Come back to the book during different seasons of your life, what speaks to you today may encourage you differently tomorrow.

5. Take action.
Wisdom only transforms when practiced. Choose one idea from each lesson and live it out. It could be showing kindness, saving money, speaking truth, or daring to dream bigger.

6. Pass it on.
The goal isn't just to learn—it's to live and to leave a legacy. Share what you've learned. Encourage someone younger or a friend who needs it. Let your growth inspire theirs.

Remember, this isn't just a book, it's a guide to help you build a life of purpose, wisdom, and faith. Read it with an open heart and let every page nudge you a little closer to the person you were created to be.

50 Things To Help You Win

In Life, Money and Relationships

Developed By Sharon D. Fiberesima
For Scribal Publishing

Contributors: Adenike Olasimbo. Angela Ohiorenoya. Emmanuel Olatokun. Ginikachukwu John Ibeagha. Joseph Omeiza. Michael Isichei. Ngozi Ketochi-Ekpo. Orifie Uyo. Otonye Inwang. Seun Omoha. Sunmbo Lizzy Olatunji. Sharon D. Fiberesima

Scribal

Scribal Publishing
London

XXVIII

Part One: Know Yourself, The Foundation of Everything

"Knowing yourself is the beginning of all wisdom."

~ Aristotle

Long before you master money, relationships, or even career choices, the most important subject you will ever study is yourself. Self-awareness is not just a motivational buzzword; research shows that people who understand their strengths and weaknesses are 32% more likely to feel satisfied in life and work (Eurich, *Harvard Business Review*, 2018).

Yet most people go through life without ever asking the big questions: *Who am I? Why am I here? What do I want? Where am I going?* These questions form the compass of your life. Without them, you may find yourself running hard in the wrong direction, achieving success in the world's eyes but feeling empty inside.

History gives us countless reminders of the power of self-understanding. Socrates, the ancient philosopher, spent his life encouraging others to "know thyself," believing that without self-knowledge, all other learning was shallow. In more recent times, leaders and innovators who changed the world—from Nelson Mandela to Maya Angelou—did so because they understood who they were and refused to let external pressure redefine them.

This section will help you pause, reflect, and begin the lifelong journey of self-discovery. It will show you why knowing your strengths, your values, and even your weaknesses is not arrogance but wisdom. It will also point you to the truth that your uniqueness is not random, it's a clue to your purpose.

To know yourself is to own your story, to embrace your God-given design, and step into the confidence that comes from living authentically.

Every other part of your growth: finances, relationships, purpose, and excellence rests on this foundation. If you can understand yourself, you can understand how to shape your future.

50 Things to Help You Win

In Life, Money & Relationships

Shaping Your Life Through Your Thoughts

A person becomes exactly who they believe they are.

The other day, I was in an Uber when the driver pressed the brakes, and the car let out this terrible, clanging sound. It was so loud that everyone around could hear. A few years ago, I had a car that made that kind of squeaky noise whenever I pressed the brakes, not nearly as bad as the Uber's though but at the time, I was always deeply embarrassed whenever it made that sound. I would always silently pray that no one I knew was nearby whenever I was going to park the car, because I was convinced they would judge me for the noise the car made.

Yet, as I sat comfortably in my Uber that day listening to a far worse noise, I felt nothing. No shame, no embarrassment, nothing! Why? Because it wasn't *my* car. The sound had nothing to do with me.

That was the moment I realised something profound: it wasn't really the sound of my car that embarrassed me years ago, it was my interpretation of it. I wasn't reacting to the noise itself but to the story I had told myself about the perception others may have developed about me because of that car. So that sound became a mirror for my own insecurity.

This is true in so many areas of life. Most of the time, it's not the actual event that shapes our feelings, but the meaning we attach to it. When someone doesn't reply your message right away, what do you think in that instant? Do you feel ignored by their lack of immediate response? A friend makes a passing comment, and you hear, *Oh, they don't like me anymore.* Often, our greatest battles are not external but internal, fought in the arena of our mind.

Psychologists call this "cognitive appraisal," meaning that the way we interpret a situation is determined by how we feel about it. Two people can go through the same experience but react in completely different ways, simply because of how they are thinking. As Marcus Aurelius, the Roman philosopher, put it, "You have power over your mind not outside events. Realise this, and you will find strength."

If you can pause for a moment, and ask yourself: *What am I thinking right now? Why does this bother me? Is it the event itself or my interpretation of it?* You will already be further ahead than most people. Many studies suggest that self-aware individuals are not only more resilient but also more successful, because they are able to manage their thoughts before those thoughts dictate their actions.

The truth is, you cannot control everything that happens to you, but you can control how you see it. That's the power of your thoughts, they affect how you feel, and those feelings shape what you do. Over time, what you do becomes the story of your life, so be careful how you think about things that happen in your life.

Wisdom in One Line: Your thoughts shape your reactions and your life.

To think about...

- What thoughts do you catch yourself repeating the most?
- How can you turn a negative thought into a positive one this week?

50 Things to Help You Win

In Life, Money & Relationships

You are Exactly Who You Were Meant to Be

"Be yourself; everyone else is already taken."
– Oscar Wilde

When I was a teenager, I often asked myself what was wrong with me. Why couldn't I just blend in like everyone else? I tried—oh, how I tried but no matter how hard I worked at fitting in, I always felt like the odd one out. *Different. Strange. Weird.*

Fast forward a few (or more than a few) years later, and I can now see the truth; those very things that made me feel out of place were not flaws but gifts. The quirks I once wanted to erase became the exact areas through which I now bring value to the world.

Here's the thing: we are not designed to be carbon copies of one another. Imagine if everyone looked the same, thought the same, acted the same way. What a colourless, boring world that would be! Instead, God in His wisdom created each of us so uniquely that no two persons on earth—dead or alive—has the same fingerprints. Our voices, abilities, and perspectives are all signs that no two lives were ever meant to be identical. You are not weird. You are a carefully designed masterpiece, made to shine in your own distinct way.

The challenge, however, is that difference can feel uncomfortable. When you don't fit neatly into the mould others expect, it's easy to believe something is wrong with you. Society often rewards conformity because it feels safe and familiar. But purpose is rarely found in blending in; it is uncovered when you dare to embrace your uniqueness.

History is filled with examples of people who were *different* and changed their world because of it. Albert Einstein struggled in school but became one of the most brilliant minds of the 20th century. Rosa Parks was just one woman on a bus, but her quiet defiance sparked a movement. Even in Scripture, David was overlooked as a young shepherd boy yet he was chosen by God to be king over the nation of Israel. None of these people fit the description, yet their difference was the key to their destiny.

So, what about you? The things you consider odd: your love for details, your creative imagination, your stubborn persistence, your deep compassion, are not accidents. They are clues to what you can do and the impact you can make. Your job is to discover them, nurture them, and let them grow. One day, you'll look back and realise you were never *weird*, you were simply different, and it's okay to be different. The world doesn't need another copy, it needs the original you.

Wisdom in One Line: Your uniqueness is your gift to the world.

To think about...

- What's one thing about yourself you used to dislike but now see as special?
- How could you use your difference to bless others?

50 Things to Help You Win

In Life, Money & Relationships

You Are So Loved

"You are loved simply because you exist."
– Mother Teresa

You are loved. Not just a little, not halfway, not sometimes, you are loved completely! By God, by your parents, by your siblings, and by the people who truly care about you. And here's something even more beautiful to remember alongside: you don't have to earn this love. You don't have to prove yourself, perform, or try to be perfect for you to be loved. You are loved because you are.

People who know they are loved act differently, think differently, show up differently because there is this confidence that comes from knowing that you are loved. You don't go begging for love or begging to be accepted because you are secure.

Look! There is only one of you in the entire world. Think about that! The Creator of the universe looked at the Earth and decided it wouldn't be complete without *you*. That's how valuable and important you are. There will never be another person exactly like you, because your uniqueness is part of the plan.

How does it feel to read that? Do you believe it? And if you don't, ask yourself why.

I get it; growing up can feel complicated. Sometimes things aren't perfect at home. Some other times you feel lost, unseen, or even invisible, while being surrounded by family and friends. It can make you question whether you're truly loved or whether you matter. But here's the truth; no matter what your circumstances look like, no matter how you feel at any moment, there is One who loves you perfectly; God.

Please hold on to that truth always. Remember it when negative thoughts creep into your mind and try to tell you otherwise. The truth remains unshaken: you are precious, you are valuable, and you are loved.

Never forget it. And whenever you do, remind yourself again.

Wisdom in One Line: You never have to earn love—you already have it.

To think about...

- Who in your life reminds you that you're loved?
- What can you do to remind yourself of this truth on hard days?

In Life, Money & Relationships

Own and Believe in Your Voice

"Speak your mind, even if your voice shakes." – Maggie Kuhn

When you know you're loved, it's easier to speak up. When I was a child, I often heard comments like, *"You're rude." "You don't know how to speak with respect." "You're too forward."* I desperately wanted to be liked and be in everybody's good books so I slowly stopped talking altogether. It felt safer at first, I mean no one scolded me for anything now that I was silent.

But soon I realised that something had happened to me. I had stopped having opinions about things. When someone asked me what I thought about something or if I liked something, I had nothing to say. By silencing my voice, I had silenced myself. A timid teenager was all that was left of the bold little girl I used to be. I, who used to be fearless, had now become the target of bullying by my classmates and I couldn't stand up for myself.

One day, I got to my breaking point – I can't say if it was the bullying, but I could no longer keep quiet. I remembered the little bold girl I used to be, and how nobody dared to bully me and decided NO MORE! Little by little, I started speaking up again.

At first my voice shook and my knees knocked, but I kept speaking. I stood up to the classmate who had bullied me and shut it down. I began sharing my thoughts in conversations. I even discovered my sense of humour again, so much so that a friend of three years at the time admitted to me that she never knew I had one. Slowly, I started reclaiming my voice, and with it, my confidence.

Here's the truth: it's easy to doubt yourself. Maybe you've thought, *What if I'm wrong? What if people laugh? What if someone else knows more than me?* That fear can keep you quiet, waiting for someone else to speak first or to permit you. But the world doesn't need another copy—it needs you. No one else sees life exactly the way you do. Your perspective, experiences, and ideas are unique, and that makes your voice valuable.

If you don't believe in your own voice, why should anyone else? Confidence doesn't suddenly appear when you feel ready; it grows every time you choose to trust that what you have to say matters. You won't always get it right. You'll make mistakes, stumble over words, and sometimes say the wrong thing. That is okay, mistakes are part of growth. Don't let the fear of imperfection silence you.

The more you speak up, the stronger your voice becomes. And you will notice something amazing; people respond more to authenticity than cowardice. They don't need you to be perfect, they need you to be real.

It's time to stop waiting for permission. Stop shrinking back or downplaying yourself to make others comfortable. Use your voice. Ask questions. Share your ideas. Stand up for yourself. Speak the truth with respect and courage. Your voice is your power, and the world needs to hear it.

Wisdom in One Line: Your voice is valuable. Own it, believe in it, and never be afraid to use it.

To think about...

- When was the last time you held back your opinion on any matter?
- What's one safe space where you can practise speaking up more?

50 Things to Help You Win

In Life, Money & Relationships

You Are Strong, You Are Bold, You Are Brave

"Courage doesn't always roar. Sometimes courage is the quiet voice at the end of the day saying, 'I will try again tomorrow.'"
– Mary Anne Radmacher

Strength doesn't always look like lifting heavy weights or winning battles. Sometimes, strength is simply daring to try. Boldness is raising your hand when no one else will. Bravery is taking a step forward, even when you feel nervous.

The truth is, you are strong, you are bold, you are brave. That a subject is hard for others does not mean it will be hard for you. That a snack is supposedly sour does not mean you will not like its taste. That people have different customs does not mean you cannot learn meaningful lessons from them.

We each carry different gifts, abilities, and strengths. What looks like a mountain to one person might be just a hill for another. That is why you should never let another person's struggle define your own limits.

People may try to discourage you from pursuing something they feel is difficult, hard, impossible or even dangerous but remember your path is different. There is room for you to try, to learn, and to succeed in your own way. The same is true when it comes to learning from other people. Just because someone in another culture, family, or nation does things differently doesn't mean they are wrong. It simply means there is more to discover in the world. The world is a rich tapestry of ideas, traditions, and wisdom. If you remain open and curious, you'll find treasures that will stretch your mind and strengthen your character.

So here's what I want you to remember: you are not ordinary. You are the child of a King—uniquely gifted, deeply loved, and designed for greatness. So be bold! Explore the many gifts God has given you, broaden your horizon, learn new things, and become all that God has called you to be.

God has placed in you gifts that no one else has. Don't hide them. Don't shrink back because others are afraid. Step into opportunities with boldness and courage. Explore your interests. Try new things. Say yes to growth!

Every new thing you attempt, every challenge you embrace, every skill you learn is shaping you into the person God created you to be. The road may not always be easy, but you are not walking it alone. Trust Him. Step out in faith. And watch how far He can take you when you choose to live strong, bold, and brave.

Wisdom in One Line: You can face challenges because of the strength within you.

To think about...

- When did you surprise yourself by being braver than you thought?
- What new challenge can you try this week?

50 Things to Help You Win

Shine Anyway

"No one turns on a light and then hides it — they put it where everyone can see it so it brightens the whole room."

Maya loved art. She would spend hours sketching, painting, and bringing her imagination to life. But at school, she kept it hidden. Her friends weren't into art, and she didn't want to seem "different." So she laughed at their jokes, followed their trends, and tucked her sketchbook away.

One day, her teacher announced an art competition. Maya's heart leapt, but doubt rushed in at the same instant. *What if they laugh? What if they think I'm trying too hard?* At lunch, she hesitated before mentioning it to her friends.

"You? Entering an art competition?" one of them said, raising an eyebrow. Another shrugged, *"It's kinda nerdy…but do what you want?"*

That night, Maya stared at her sketchbook, caught between fear and desire. Then she remembered something her grandmother once told her: *"No one lights a candle just to hide it under a basket. If God gave you a gift, it's meant to shine."*

With trembling hands but a determined heart, Maya signed up. Some friends rolled their eyes, but others were curious to see what she would come up with.

When her artwork was displayed at school, guess what? People noticed her ingenuity. They admired her creativity, encouraged her, and even asked for tips on how they could start drawing.

That was the moment Maya realised something powerful: the right people will never ask you to shrink. They'll celebrate your light. And those who mock or walk away? That's okay. You don't need to make yourself smaller to be loved by people who don't have an appreciation for what makes you different.

We all have gifts: talents, passions, and strengths that make us unique. But fear of other people's judgment often convinces us to hide them. We worry about being "too much," standing out, or drawing attention. Yet the world doesn't need dimmed-down versions of us. It needs us in all of our brightness.

It doesn't matter what your gift is: art, music, writing, leadership, kindness, problem-solving, don't bury it or try to reduce its impact. Express it fully. Express it confidently. Because when you choose to shine, you not only step into the fullness of who God made you to be—you also give others permission to shine too.

Wisdom in One Line: Never shrink to fit in—shine anyway, because your light was made to be seen.

To think about...

- Is there a gift or talent you've been hiding?
- What's one small way you could "shine" this week?

50 Things to Help You Win

In Life, Money & Relationships

Growth is a Process

"Little by little, day by day, what is meant for you will find its way."
– Unknown

When I was a little girl, I couldn't wait to grow up. I thought adulthood was the golden ticket to freedom, the moment I could finally do what I wanted and be who I wanted to be without restrictions. Back then, I believed that growing up was a destination, a place you arrive at and stay forever. What I didn't realise was that growth is not a final stop; it's a lifelong process. As long as we are alive, we are to keep growing.

The mistake I made was equating growth with age, but age alone doesn't guarantee maturity. That's why you sometimes see adults behaving like children: throwing tantrums, being selfish, or avoiding responsibility. They may have grown in years, but not in wisdom or emotional strength.

That's why it's important not to rush through life. Don't be in such a hurry to "grow up" that you miss the treasures of the season you're in right now. Childhood and the teenage years are very precious, and you only experience them once. Each stage of life has its lessons, its joys, and its opportunities to shape you into the person you're becoming.

I know it can feel frustrating when you're young and so many decisions are made for you by the adults in your life. Chances are you might feel powerless or stuck, waiting for the day you can finally take control of your own life.

But here's a secret: no one, not even adults have complete control over their lives. Grown-ups may seem to have more choices, but they also face more responsibilities. Bills decide how money is spent. Governments set rules for what people can and can't do. Family and work responsibilities place demands on time and energy. Freedom comes with age, yes but it comes also with the weight of responsibility. That's why maturity is very important.

True growth isn't just about getting older; it's about becoming stronger inside. Part of growth is learning how to manage your emotions so they don't control you. It requires developing your mind so you can make wiser decisions. It entails nurturing your relationship with God and learning how to treat others with love and respect. Growth is about building character, resilience, and maturity little by little.

Growth shows up in the small things: how you react when someone upsets you, how you treat your friends, how you handle conflict at home, how you dedicate yourself to learning, even when it's tough. These little choices, made consistently, are what slowly shape you into a balanced, stable adult.

Note this: growth takes time. You don't have to get everything right at once so be patient with yourself. Growth is not a sprint; it's a lifelong journey. Every mistake, every challenge, every new lesson is part of the process.

So keep growing. Keep learning. Keep becoming. You are a work in progress, and that's exactly as it should be.

Wisdom in One Line: Life is about growing daily, not rushing to a destination.

To think about...

- What's something you're still learning that requires patience?
- How do you remind yourself that it's okay not to have it all figured out yet?

50 Things to Help You Win

In Life, Money & Relationships

Seek Transformation Above Popularity

"Don't aim for success if you want it; just do what you love and believe in, and it will come naturally."
– David Frost

We live in a world where popularity often looks like the ultimate prize. Social media counts your worth in likes and followers, peer pressure pushes you to fit in, and entertainment makes fame look like the highest goal. But here's the truth: popularity is temporary. It can fade in a moment, but growth, wisdom, and transformation last a lifetime.

One of the greatest gifts God has given you is the ability to learn and keep learning. Every time you read, ask questions, or stretch yourself to understand something new, you grow stronger inside. That growth transforms you. And transformation is far more valuable than recognition because it changes who you are not just how others see you.

Think about it. When the world faces problems: hunger, injustice, leadership crises, people don't go looking for who's the most famous. They look for people who are wise, knowledgeable, and capable of solving real problems. Leaders who transform nations, inventors who change industries, and mentors who guide others don't need popularity to make an impact. They need wisdom, discipline, and growth.

Here's the secret: when you focus on transformation, recognition often follows naturally. People will notice your character, your wisdom, and your skills, not because you tried to impress them, but because you became someone worth following.

So instead of chasing likes, chase growth. Instead of craving attention, crave wisdom. Read books. Learn from people who are wiser than you. Be curious. Be open to correction. Keep developing yourself.

Popularity may win you applause today, but transformation will prepare you to make a difference tomorrow. And that difference—changing lives, solving problems, and becoming the best version of yourself—is far more powerful than fame could ever be.

Wisdom in One Line: Growth lasts longer than applause.

To think about...

- Do you care more about likes or about growth?
- What's one way you could focus on transformation this week?

In Life, Money & Relationships

Your Biggest Job in Life is to Understand Yourself

"The unexamined life is not worth living."
– Socrates

The one person you will never escape is *you*. You wake up with yourself, go to bed with yourself, and carry yourself everywhere you go. No one will ever know you the way you do or at least, the way you *could*—if you take the time to understand yourself truly.

But here's the problem: most people never do. Studies suggest that most people, over 70%, go through life without ever stopping to ask the deeper questions. They go to school, get jobs, get married, have children, pay bills, and run through the motions of life. They're busy, but not fulfilled. Productive, but not purposeful. Alive, but not truly living.

That's because they've never paused to wrestle with four of the most important questions every human being should ask:

- **Who am I?** (Identity)
- **Why am I here?** (Purpose)
- **What do I want?** (Vision)
- **Where am I going?** (Goals)

A life without these answers is like sailing without a compass, you may be moving, but you don't know where you'll end up.

I know this because I lived it. For years, I did everything society told me to do. I studied, worked, ticked off milestones, and followed the script of what was "expected." Yet, in the year I turned 38, I came dangerously close to a breakdown. I had achieved everything on paper, but inside, I was restless and empty. Why? Because I had never stopped to ask myself those four questions.

That season forced me to dig deep. It wasn't easy, but beginning to answer those questions gave me back my life. For the first time, I felt a sense of clarity, direction, and peace. I discovered that true success isn't about ticking off society's boxes; it's about living from a place of self-understanding and purpose.

Now, I won't pretend this journey is simple. These aren't questions you answer overnight. Sometimes you'll need wise voices: that of mentors, counsellors, trusted guides to help you along the way. What matters most is that you don't avoid the questions. You will have to face them eventually, and the earlier you do, the better.

Why not start today? Begin paying attention to yourself: your strengths, your weaknesses, your passions, your struggles. Listen to what excites you, what drains you, what matters deeply to you.

Bit by bit, you'll uncover the real you. And when you do, you'll find that understanding yourself is not only your biggest job in life, it's also the greatest gift you can give yourself and the world.

Wisdom in One Line: Knowing who you are sets the direction of your life.

To think about...

- Which of the four big questions (Who am I? Why am I here? What do I want? Where am I going?) feels most important to you right now?
- How could you start exploring your answer?

50 Things to Help You Win

In Life, Money & Relationships

Mastering Your Emotions

"A foolish person lets all their anger and feelings explode, but a wise person stays calm and keeps control." – King Solomon

Emotions are part of what makes us human. You can feel happy one moment and lonely the next, excited today and anxious tomorrow. That's normal. But here's what you need to know: your emotions are not the same as your identity. Feeling sad doesn't mean you are a "sad person." Feeling angry doesn't mean you're doomed to be angry forever. Emotions are like visitors, they come and go.

The real question is: what do you do with them while they're here?

That's where **self-control** comes in. Self-control is the ability to pause, breathe, and choose your response instead of letting your feelings take over. For example, when you're angry, your first instinct may be to lash out or say something mean, slam a door, or even hit someone. But self-control helps you stop and think: *Will this line of action help or make things worse?*

The same is true with sadness. It's okay to feel sad, but don't let that sadness take over your entire day or shape your decisions. Remember your feelings are temporary. They won't last forever.

Sometimes the best thing you can do is share how you're feeling with God in prayer, or talk to a trusted friend, mentor, or adult. Expressing your emotions in a healthy way lightens the load and helps you process them more clearly.

And here's something else: how you treat others while being emotional matters. It's easy to push people away or snap at them when you're upset, but choosing kindness even when you don't feel like it, is a real sign of strength. Anyone can act out when they're angry. It takes courage and maturity to remain calm and respectful.

Mastering your emotions doesn't mean ignoring them or pretending they don't exist. It means acknowledging them without letting them control your actions. The more you practise this, the stronger and wiser you'll become. Remember this when next your emotions feel overwhelming: you are in charge. Your feelings are part of you, but they neither define nor control you unless you let them.

Wisdom in One Line: Feelings are real, but they don't have to rule you.

To think about...

- Which emotion is hardest for you to control—anger, sadness, or worry?
- What's one healthy way you can handle it next time it shows up?

When you know who you are, you also begin to understand how to steward what you have. Identity gives direction, but responsibility gives stability. That's why the next part turns to money; not as a master, but as a tool. By learning how to handle money early, you give yourself freedom later and create opportunities to live out the uniqueness you've discovered in yourself.

50 Things to Help You Win

Part Two: Money Matters, Understanding Finance Early

"Financial literacy is not an option; it is a survival skill."
~ Alan Greenspan

Money may seem like a grown-up issue, but learning how it works early in life is one of the greatest advantages you can give yourself. Studies show that only 24% of millennials demonstrate basic financial literacy (National Financial Educators Council, 2023). Even more concerning is that many adults live with heavy debt simply because they were never taught the principles of budgeting, saving, or investing when young.

History tells us that wealth is rarely accidental; it is usually the result of discipline, wise stewardship, and understanding opportunities. From ancient merchants along the Silk Road who learned to reinvest their profits, to innovators like Benjamin Franklin who famously said, 'An investment in knowledge pays the best interest,' those who learned to manage resources changed not only their lives but the lives of generations after them.

This section will help you understand money as a tool, not a master. It will show you how to think about money wisely, how to use it to create value, and how to ensure you control your finances rather than letting them control you.

In Life, Money & Relationships

Learn about Money as Early as Possible

"The sooner you start learning about money, the sooner money will start working for you."
– Unknown

Financial literacy sounds like a big thing, but it is just about understanding how money works and the earlier you learn this, the better.

My dear father—God rest his soul—in a bid to protect us as children, would never give us allowances for the week or month (where we could have learned to manage our money), he would rather insist on giving us allowance every morning to make sure we had money for break time in school that day. Even when we got to the university, he would insist that we come home every Sunday to receive our allowance and refused to let us have it every month, as most of our colleagues did.

Though it was well-intentioned, his methods prevented my brothers and I from learning how to manage money, and we're all still struggling with that to this day. I for one, had to pay for a financial literacy class in my late thirties, just to get a hang of my finances.

It's not too early to learn the basics (and more) of money; to learn what is a need and what is a want? What a budget is and how to create one? How much of one's income (or allowance) should be spent and how much should go into savings? What is an investment and how can you get started investing as early as possible?

Part of financial literacy is recognizing your abilities and talents, and finding ways to package them as a marketable product or service that can bring in money. Is this something you want to build a career on or is it going to be a side-business? All of these are questions and conversations that you can begin to have now.

What you are doing is creating a future for yourself that you can be proud of tomorrow. I promise, you will be glad if you learn about money and start practicing what you learn as early as possible.

Wisdom in One Line: Becoming wise about money early in life will give you freedom when you get older.

To think about...

- What's one thing about money you wish you understood better?
- How can you practise managing money, even in small amounts?

In Life, Money & Relationships

Solve Problems, Create Value

"Wealth is created by solving problems for others."
– Naval Ravikant

Have you ever thought about what money really represents? At its core, money is often a reward for solving problems. Every job, every business, and every invention exists because someone identified a need and developed a solution.

When you're hungry, you head to a restaurant where someone has solved the problem of food preparation. When you're cold, you put on a coat that someone designed to solve the problem of warmth. Even the phone in your hand is the result of thousands of people solving different problems, from communication to design to technology. And in return for these solutions provided, people make money.

That's why one of the smartest ways to think about money is to connect it with value. The bigger or more helpful the solution, the greater the reward can be.

Start small. Look around your neighbourhood, school, or family. Is there a neighbour who needs help with gardening? A classmate struggling with homework? Parents who would pay someone to babysit or tutor? Each of these is an opportunity to not only show kindness but also to practice the skill of problem-solving.

Ask yourself often: *How can I make life easier or better for someone else?* You'll be surprised at how many doors open when you think this way. People will happily pay for things that save them time, effort, or energy. Whether it's mowing the grass, washing cars, designing digital art, or even selling homemade crafts, these small steps build both your confidence and your earning potential.

As you grow, your ability to solve problems can scale up. The more creative, unique, and valuable your solutions are, the more opportunities you will find—not just to earn money but to make a lasting impact.

So, don't just wait for money to appear. Train your eyes to see problems as opportunities. Act, solve them well, and watch how value and reward follows.

Wisdom in One Line: Money comes as a reward for solving problems.

To think about...

- What problem at school or at home could you help solve right now?
- How might that solution also create opportunities for you?

In Life, Money & Relationships

Save and Invest: Money is a Seed

"Plant your money like a seed—watch it grow into a tree."

Imagine you were hungry and had some seed in your hand. If you ate it, it would solve the problem of hunger and you would be momentarily satisfied. However, those seeds once eaten, are gone forever. But what if you planted the seed, watered and cared for it? That little seed can grow into a big tree that produces fruit again and again.

Money works the same way! If you spend it all the moment you get it, it's gone. But if you save and invest, your money can grow over time and even earn more money for you.

Saving simply means putting money aside for something important later. You might want to save for a new bike, a trip, or even University.

Investing takes it a step further. When you invest, you let your money work for you. You can invest your money for example, to buy tools to start dog walking or lawn mowing. The money spent will create something that can earn even more money. Or, when you're older, you might invest in things like stocks or property, which grow in value over time. The sooner you start saving and investing, the more your "money tree" will grow.

You will need to be patient though because just like waiting for a seed to grow into a tree, it takes time and care. But when your tree begins to bring fruit (profit), it would be worth the effort.

Wisdom in One Line: Plant money like a seed so it grows into more.

To think about...

- What's something you'd like to save up for this year?
- If your money were a seed, how could you "plant" it so it grows?

Be Generous: Look for Ways to Give

"We make a living by what we get, but we make a life by what we give."
– Winston Churchill

One of the most wonderful things about money is the chance to use it to help others. Have you ever seen someone in need and wished you could do something about it?

When you're generous, you discover that even small acts can bring joy and make a real difference in someone's life. A donation to a food bank can feed a family for a day. Buying a simple gift can brighten a friend's week. Giving to a charity you believe in can help them achieve their goals.

Generosity is powerful because it multiplies—what seems small to you can be a huge blessing to someone else.

But generosity isn't just about giving money away. It starts with recognising how much you already have. Gratitude makes you more aware of your blessings, and generosity is gratitude in action. It's not about emptying your wallet; it's about sharing a portion of what you have to help someone in need.

A simple way to practise is to set aside a small percentage of every pound you receive—whether it's an allowance, pocket money, or pay from a part-time job just for giving. This way, you're always prepared when an opportunity to help comes along.

The amazing thing is that generosity doesn't only change the world, it changes you. It shifts your mindset from "What can I get?" to "What can I give?" It reminds you that money isn't just for keeping or spending; it's a tool to spread kindness, joy, and hope. Generosity helps you become more compassionate, more grateful, and more aware of others.

So, the next time you receive money, pause and ask yourself: *"How can I use part of this to help someone else?"* You'd be surprised at how much lighter and happier your heart feels when you live with open hands.

Wisdom in One Line: Money is more meaningful when it's used to bring joy and hope to others—so always look for ways to give.

To think about...

- Who around you could use kindness or help right now?
- What's one small way you can give this week?

In Life, Money & Relationships

Be Content with What You Have Now

Strive to be better but be thankful for what you have now.

Life is full of dreams, goals, and desires; and that's a good thing. Ambition keeps you moving forward. But along the way, it's just as important to pause and appreciate where you are right now. That's what contentment is all about.

Contentment doesn't mean giving up or settling for less than you're capable of. Instead, it means finding satisfaction in your current season while still working, hoping, and praying for more. It's choosing to see the blessings you already have instead of constantly chasing what you think you lack.

The danger of discontentment is comparison. When you spend too much time looking at what other people have; whether it's their clothes, their grades, their popularity, or their opportunities, you risk falling into a cycle of dissatisfaction. You start wishing your life looked like theirs and forget that your journey has its own timing and purpose.

The truth is, comparison steals joy. It breeds jealousy and can even lead to feelings of inadequacy or depression. It blinds you to the progress you've already made and the gifts you've already been given. And it distracts you from the unique path God has designed for you.

Instead, **learn to cultivate gratitude**. Gratitude is a powerful tool; it shifts your focus from what's missing to what's present. It reminds you that even small victories are worth celebrating. Gratitude doesn't cancel out your dreams; it simply keeps your heart at peace while you pursue them.

Every season of your life has value. The lessons you learn now will prepare you for the opportunities of tomorrow. True joy doesn't come from endlessly accumulating more; it comes from recognising the beauty of the present and trusting God for the future.

So celebrate where you are. Be thankful for what you have. And let that joy fuel your determination to keep growing. Gratitude and contentment are not weaknesses; they are strengths that will carry you into living a purposeful and fulfilled life.

Wisdom in One Line: Gratitude for today prepares you for tomorrow.

To think about...

- What's one thing you're grateful for today?
- How can you stop comparing yourself to others in that area?

In Life, Money & Relationships

Value the Labour of Others

"No work is insignificant. All work that is honest deserves respect."
– Unknown

It is important to honour and appreciate the labour and efforts of others. Never devalue someone's hard work simply because you want to pay less or because you fail to see the full extent of their contribution. Every skill, talent, and effort is valuable, even if it isn't something you personally can't relate to. What you are unable to do for yourself must be respected, and the abilities others bring to the table should be celebrated rather than undermined.

When you dismiss or belittle someone's labour, it reflects more on your character than on the value of their work. It is unjust to take advantage of others' skills or talents, whether by undervaluing them, refusing fair compensation, or withholding credit. Running down someone's efforts to elevate your own is not only unkind but ultimately diminishes the joy and dignity of meaningful work.

Recognise that every person's gift is unique and vital. As the saying goes, "The gift of a man makes way for him." By celebrating and acknowledging the work and talents of others, you not only encourage them but also contribute to a culture of mutual respect and collaboration.

True success comes when we celebrate others and give credit where it is due. So, whether it's a craft, a service, or a skill, take the time to honour the labour of others. Doing so reflects gratitude, humility, and a heart that values humanity.

Wisdom in One Line: Respect the effort and skill behind every service.

To think about...

- Who do you sometimes take for granted, even though they work hard?
- How can you show respect or appreciation to them this week?

In Life, Money & Relationships

Stewardship: Avoid Debt and Use Money Wisely

The person who borrows is always at the mercy of the lender.
– King Solomon

Jason loved sneakers. When a new limited-edition pair came out, all his friends were buzzing about it. The problem was Jason didn't have enough money. Instead of waiting and saving, he borrowed from his cousin, promising to pay it back "soon." At first, Jason felt amazing walking into school with his fresh kicks. But within weeks, the excitement wore off. Meanwhile, his cousin kept reminding him about the money he owed. Jason had to hand over every bit of allowance and skip outings with his friends just to pay back the debt. The sneakers that once made him feel cool now just made him feel trapped.

That's exactly what debt does. It gives you something quickly but steals your peace and freedom in the long run. When you owe, you're not in control of your money; it belongs to someone else before it even reaches your pocket.

Instead of falling into that trap, practice wise stewardship. Stewardship means being responsible with what you've been given. Learn to spot the difference between needs (things you must have) and wants (things you can wait for). Saving teaches patience, and it gives you freedom—freedom to buy without guilt, freedom to say yes to opportunities, and freedom to live without the stress of debt.

Using money wisely doesn't mean you cannot enjoy life. It means you're intentional. You spend with foresight, you save for what matters, and you give in ways that bring joy. Wise stewardship sets you up not just for financial stability but for peace of mind.

So the next time you're tempted to borrow for something shiny, remember Jason's sneakers. Ask yourself: *Is this worth the trap of debt, or can I wait and save for it the wise way?*

Wisdom in One Line: Debt is a trap so manage money with care and foresight.

To think about...

- What's a purchase you want? Do you think it's a need or a want?
- How can you practise saving instead of borrowing?

In Life, Money & Relationships

Entrepreneurship: Start Small, Think Big

"Don't look down on small starts — God is happy to see you take the first step."

When Amir was fourteen, he noticed his classmates often forgot their pens and pencils. Instead of just lending his, he decided to bring extras from home and sell them at a small profit. At first, it was just a few pens here and there, but soon people started coming to him because they knew he always had what they needed. By the end of the term, Amir had saved enough money to buy a second-hand bicycle; something his parents couldn't have afforded at the time.

That's the power of entrepreneurship. It often begins with something simple, ordinary, even small. You don't need millions or a huge office to start. What you need is an eye for opportunities, the courage to act, and the patience to grow.

Starting small teaches you valuable lessons; how to manage money, deal with people, and solve problems. It also builds resilience, because mistakes are easier (and cheaper) to fix when you're just beginning. But while you start small, never think small. Dream beyond where you are. Imagine what your idea could become in five years, ten years, or even a lifetime.

Every big company you see today: Apple, Nike, Amazon, all started as a small idea, often in someone's garage or bedroom. What made the difference was that the people behind them thought big, kept learning, and refused to give up.

So don't wait until you're older or until you have "enough money" to start something. Look around, what do you see people need? How can you meet that need? Begin small, stay consistent, and keep your vision big.

Wisdom in One Line: Start small today, but let your dreams reach far beyond tomorrow.

To think about...

- If you could start a tiny business today, what would it be?
- What's one small step you could take to begin?

In Life, Money & Relationships

Money can open doors, but it cannot fill your heart. True joy comes from the people you walk with: family, friends, mentors, and communities that sharpen and support you. Having laid the groundwork of financial wisdom, the next part focuses on building relationships that last, because wealth without love is empty, but love shared enriches everything.

50 Things to Help You Win

Part Three: People & Relationships – Building Connections That Last

"No man is an island, entire of itself; every man is a piece of the continent."
– John Donne

Life is richer when shared. Relationships with family, friends, mentors, and communities are the soil in which we grow. Social scientists tell us that the quality of our relationships is the single biggest predictor of long-term happiness and health (Harvard Study of Adult Development, 1938–present, the longest study of human well-being).

History gives countless examples: great leaders and reformers from Martin Luther King Jr. to Mother Teresa were never alone in their impact. They were supported, encouraged, and sharpened by communities of people who believed in the same vision. Even in the Bible, King David had Jonathan, and Paul had Timothy.

This section explores what it means to be loved, to love others, to choose friends wisely, and to navigate the sometimes challenging dynamics of family and community. At its heart, it will remind you that success without relationships is empty, but even modest achievements become deeply fulfilling when shared with those you love.

In Life, Money & Relationships

Never Beg for Love or Acceptance

"Don't waste your energy trying to change opinions...Do your thing, and don't care if they like it."
– Tina Fey

As you grow older, you'll notice friendships, groups, and relationships starting to matter more. You might begin to feel that pull to fit in, to be noticed, to be loved. That's completely normal but here's what you must always have at the back of your mind: **you are already valuable, just as you are.**

Your worth is not something you always have to earn. You don't have to change yourself, perform, or beg for anyone's attention or affection. You are worthy of love, kindness, and respect simply because you exist. God created you intentionally, and that alone makes you priceless.

Sadly, not everyone will see your worth. Some people may withhold kindness, try to make you feel small, or treat you like you don't belong. It's tempting to think, *If I just try harder, maybe they'll like me.* But here's the truth: anyone who makes you beg for love or friendship is not someone you should want close to your heart or in your life.

The same goes for groups or relationships. If it feels off, if it leaves you drained, insecure, or feeling less of yourself; don't ignore that feeling. Your instincts are often a warning sign that something isn't right. Respect yourself enough to re-evaluate that relationship and walk away, even if it's hard. That's not weakness—it's strength.

Real love and real friendship never demand that you shrink, beg, or compromise on your values. The right people will value you for who you truly are. They will build you up, not tear you down. And when you choose to walk away from what isn't good for you, you'll look back one day with pride, knowing you protected your heart and honoured your worth.

Bottom line, never beg someone to love you. You don't need to prove your value. You already have it. Surround yourself with those who see it, celebrate it, and cherish it.

Wisdom in One Line: You deserve respect and kindness without begging for it.

To think about...

- Have you ever felt like you had to "earn" someone's friendship?
- How can you remind yourself that you're already valuable?

In Life, Money & Relationships

Respect Everyone

"Respect is how to treat everyone, not just those you want to impress."
– Richard Branson

People often say that respect is earned. Actually, it's the other way around; disrespect is earned. You should not wait for a person to earn your respect before you choose to respect them.

The dictionary defines respect as being polite, showing honour and care to someone or something you think is important. Everyone is important, so it is good behaviour to be courteous to everyone you meet. Show care to people and do not hurt their feelings. When you meet people, greet them.

A simple "good morning" or "hello" shows respect. You do not always have to wait for the other person to greet you first, especially if they are older. Always say *"thank you," "please,"* and *"I'm sorry,"* when the occasion requires it.

Showing gratitude is a sign of respect and shows that you honour that person and what they have done for you. If a person cares enough about you to go out of their way to do you a favour, it is only right to say *"thank you."*

Also, it is important to know that no one owes you anything. Even when you are asking for what you think is your right, a simple "please" will not cost you anything and it shows that you care about the other person's feelings.

Somehow, saying *sorry* is so hard for people, particularly when you feel like you did not do anything wrong. This is not to say that you should be in a hurry to accept blame for what you didn't do. But, if you are ever in a situation where you discover that you are in the wrong, waste no time in apologising. It will not cost you anything but can save a lot of trouble later.

Respecting someone means not forcing your opinions on that person. It is okay for people to disagree with you. Not everyone will see life the same way you do, and that's okay. Just because your friend does not want to play the same sport or do the same thing as you, does not mean you can't still be good friends. We are all made differently, and we like different things.

Wisdom in One Line: Respect everyone. The respect you show to others usually comes back to you as respect.

To think about...

- How do you usually show respect to others?
- What's one simple way you can show more respect this week?

In Life, Money & Relationships

Respect Yourself

"If you want to be respected by others, the great thing is to respect yourself. Only by that, only by self-respect will you compel others to respect you."
– Fyodor Dostoyevsky

As much as you need to show respect and care to everyone who comes your way, it should never be at the expense of your self-respect. Understand that respecting yourself does not mean that you are proud. It just means that you are also important, and you care about your feelings.

One of the ways you can respect yourself is through your personal hygiene. Keep yourself clean; have a shower every day, use deodorants, and moisturise your body. Ensure that your hair and clothes are clean and neat. Polish your shoes if they need polishing. Taking care of yourself is a sign that you respect yourself.

Another way to respect yourself is to respect your opinions. While you do not need to force your opinion on anyone, you should be confident of what you think. Do not let anyone shut you up or make you believe that your perspective (the way you see things) is inferior or not important. Speak your mind, and if people believe and accept what you say, fine. If they don't, that's okay too.

You are special. You do not have to do anything to be special; you were made that way. **Do not ever beg anyone to love you.** It is okay to go out of your way for others but also consider your needs. You are the only one who truly understands what you need and how to take care of yourself, so please, take care of yourself.

Do not compromise your beliefs just to please another person. If your gut instinct tells you what you are doing is wrong and against your personal beliefs, then don't do it regardless of who may get offended. Stay true to what you know is right. If you change your mind, let it be because of your conviction and not because someone persuaded you otherwise.

For example, if you have a belief that taking alcohol is wrong, then do not take a sip of alcohol just because you want to make someone happy. Again, if you have decided to wait until marriage before having sex, that is your personal conviction. Do not throw it away because you want to please a boyfriend or girlfriend.

Wisdom in One Line: Respect yourself because you are valuable. You matter, and so do your beliefs, convictions and life experiences.

To think about...

- What does respecting yourself look like in daily life?
- Is there a boundary you need to set to protect your self-respect?

In Life, Money & Relationships

Choose Your Friends Carefully

"You are the average of the five people you spend the most time with."
– Jim Rohn

What that means is that you have the final say on who becomes your friend. You are not obliged to be friends with someone just because they want to be your friend. Do not let anyone pressure you into forming a friendship.

One secret many young people don't know about friendships is that your friends have more influence on you than you are aware of. You probably know someone who was top of their class, then they made friends with someone, or some people and their grades began dropping.

You cannot hang around people with bad character all day and expect that yours won't start looking like theirs. No matter how well behaved you are, you will eventually begin to act like that friend with a bad attitude. But it goes beyond that.

Some people had great destinies. They could have been doctors, lawyers, teachers, or aerospace engineers. They could have been the very best they were capable of being. Instead, they ended up in a deadbeat job, getting drunk and living hopeless lives. Several factors could have contributed, however, if you look hard enough, you might trace their misfortune to wrong friendships.

If you surround yourself with mean friends who do not care about studying or putting in the work necessary for a bright future, then you will slowly realise that you are also adopting their attitude. On the flip side, when you keep kind friends who have good values, they will inspire you to be the kind of person you can be proud of.

But how can you tell the difference between good and bad friends? There are several indices you can use, and an important one is to see if their values align with yours. Values are the things that help you know what is right and wrong. They guide how you act, treat others, and make decisions. If you value kindness, then a person who is always unkind to others does not share your values, and you might want to think twice before becoming their friend.

Pray about your friendships. Do not be in a hurry to make friends with anyone. You can ask God to choose your friends for you because at the end of the day, you do not know a person's heart, and sometimes, it isn't always easy to tell who will make a good or bad friend.

No matter what you do, remember that you always have the right to choose. You can say "No" to a friendship that does not align with your values.

Wisdom in One Line: The company you keep shapes the person you become.

To think about...

- What qualities do you value most in a friend?
- Do your current friends encourage or distract you from being your best?

50 Things to Help You Win

In Life, Money & Relationships

Forgive Quickly and Fully

"Bear with each other and forgive one another if any of you has a grievance against someone. Forgive as the Lord forgave you."
– St. Paul

It's tempting to hold on to a grudge. Maybe your friend said something mean, and even though they've apologised, you can't stop replaying it in your mind. Maybe it's your sibling who borrowed something without asking, or a classmate who embarrassed you in front of others. When people we love and trust hurt us, the hurt cuts deep. And sometimes, staying angry unfortunately feels easier than letting go.

But here's the truth: **forgiveness is not only about the other person; it's about you**.

When you hold a grudge, you chain yourself to that moment of pain. Every time you see the person who offended you, it's like the wound gets ripped open afresh. The bitterness grows heavier with time, weighing you down, stealing your peace, and blocking your joy.

Think of it like carrying around a heavy backpack filled with rocks. Each rock represents a grudge, a disappointment, or an offense you refuse to release. At first, you might manage, but over time, the weight becomes unbearable. Forgiveness is like setting down that backpack.

Suddenly, you're lighter, freer, and able to walk forward without dragging the past with you.

Now, forgiveness doesn't mean pretending the hurt never happened. It doesn't mean excusing bad behaviour or saying it was okay. Forgiveness simply means choosing not to let anger control you anymore. It's the decision to release the burden so you can breathe again.

When you forgive, you make room for healing. You invite peace and joy back into your heart. And here's the beautiful part: forgiveness is not weakness—it's strength. It takes courage to let go when holding on feels easier.

So, instead of clinging to bitterness, choose freedom. Choose forgiveness. It's one of the strongest, bravest, and healthiest things you can do for yourself and for your future.

Wisdom in One Line: Forgiveness sets you free more than anyone else.

To think about...

- Is there someone you need to forgive right now?
- How would forgiving them free your heart?

Conflict Resolution: Learn to Talk It Out

"A gentle answer turns away wrath, but a harsh word stirs up anger."
– King Solomon

Amanda and her best friend Kemi had been inseparable since primary school. But one day, a misunderstanding over a borrowed hoodie spiralled into a full-blown argument. They stopped talking, started avoiding each other, and soon their whole group of friends was caught in the tension. Weeks passed, and Amanda felt miserable, but she was too proud to speak first. Finally, their teacher encouraged them to sit down and talk. At first, it was awkward, but as they listened to each other, they realised the whole fight had been based on assumptions. Once they talked it out, the friendship was restored, stronger than before.

Conflict is a normal part of life. Disagreements happen: between friends, siblings, classmates, even parents and children. The real question is: *How do you handle it?* Bottling things up or lashing out only makes situations worse. The healthiest way forward is to communicate: honestly, respectfully, and calmly.

Talking it out doesn't mean you'll always agree, but it helps you understand where the other person is coming from. It shows maturity when you can listen without interrupting, explain your feelings without yelling, and look for a solution instead of trying to "win" the argument.

Learning to resolve conflict is a life skill. It protects friendships, builds trust, and makes you a better leader. And the earlier you practise it, the easier it becomes to handle bigger disagreements later in life.

So, when the next conflict arises, resist the urge to stay silent or explode. Choose the better way; talk it out.

Wisdom in One Line: Problems shrink when people talk with respect.

To think about...

- Do you usually avoid conflict or face it head-on?
- What's one step you can take to handle conflict more calmly?

In Life, Money & Relationships

Digital Friendships and Social Media Boundaries

You can do whatever you want, but not everything is actually good for you.

Sophie loved connecting with people online. She had hundreds of followers and spent hours chatting, posting, and scrolling. One day, a new "friend" she met in a group chat began asking very personal questions and pressuring her to share pictures she wasn't comfortable with. At first, Sophie thought it was harmless, but soon she realised the conversations were making her uneasy. When she finally set boundaries and blocked the person, she felt relieved; like she had taken back her freedom.

That's the reality of digital friendships: they can be fun, encouraging, and even inspiring, but without boundaries, they can quickly turn harmful. Social media is powerful, it allows you to connect with people across the world, but it also exposes you to risks like comparison, peer pressure, and unsafe relationships.

Setting healthy boundaries is non-negotiable in managing digital connections. Decide what you will share and what you won't. Protect your private information. Don't measure your worth by likes, comments, or followers. And remember that not everyone online is who they claim to be.

Digital friendships should add to your life, not drain it. True friends, whether online or offline should respect your space, your values, and your "no." If a digital connection pressures you, disrespects you, or makes you feel unsafe, it's okay to step back, unfollow, or block. That's not weakness, it's wisdom.

Social media should be a tool you control, not something that controls you. Use it to learn, to grow, to encourage, and to stay connected while keeping your boundaries in place.

Wisdom in One Line: Online or offline, real friends respect your boundaries.

To think about...

- How does social media make you feel after you've been scrolling?
- What boundary could make your online time healthier?

In Life, Money & Relationships

Have Trusted Advisors

"Your plans can fall apart if you don't get advice, but when you listen to others, you're more likely to succeed."
– King Solomon

It's easy to think that your parents are just "not cool," always trying to cramp your style. Maybe it feels like all they do is nag or say no. And while that might be frustrating, here's the truth: you still need people in your life who are older, wiser, and trustworthy. People who can guide you with the kind of wisdom that only comes from experience.

The temptation is to lean only on your friends. After all, they're the ones who "get you" and understand what you're going through, right? But here's the thing, if you and your friends are about the same age, then you're likely dealing with the same challenges at the same mental level. They may mean well, and they might even share helpful experiences from their siblings or from online sources, but the reality is, they don't yet have the wisdom and life experience you really need to make the best decisions.

So, what should you do? Start by finding someone older who is trustworthy; someone you can speak honestly with and who will give you good advice. Yes, it may feel awkward to put yourself out there, but the right advisor is like gold. Their insight can save you from mistakes, encourage you when you feel lost, and point you toward opportunities you might have missed.

Where can you find these trusted advisors? Look around you. A teacher who genuinely cares. A youth group leader or counsellor. An aunt, uncle, or older family friend. And yes, don't dismiss your parents completely. Even if they nag (and they probably will sometimes), it's usually because they love you and want the best for you. You might be surprised by how much wisdom they can offer if you're open to it.

The most important thing is this: make sure you have at least one older, reliable, and trustworthy person in your corner. Someone you can talk to openly, someone who listens, and someone whose advice you know is worth following.

If you don't already have such a person in your life, start looking today. Don't wait until you're in a tough situation and feel stuck. Build those relationships now, and you'll be glad you did.

Wisdom in One Line: Seek guidance from those wiser than you.

To think about...

- Who is an older, wiser person you can talk to about life decisions?
- What's one question you'd like to ask them this month?

Relationships give us belonging, but resilience gives us strength. Even with love around you, life will test your confidence, character, and endurance. That's why the journey now shifts inward again to self-worth and resilience. These qualities help you bounce back, stand firm, and keep growing, no matter what challenges or mistakes come your way.

50 Things to Help You Win

Part Four: Growing in Self-Worth and Resilience

"You owe yourself the same kindness and care that you freely give to others."
– Unknown

Every journey of excellence begins with the way you see yourself. Before you can lead, achieve, or pursue purpose, you must first understand your value and invest in your personal growth. Too often, we think self-love is vanity or selfishness, but in truth, it is the foundation for resilience, confidence, and balanced relationships.

Research from the *Journal of Personality and Social Psychology* shows that individuals with healthy self-esteem are more likely to bounce back from setbacks, form stronger connections, and pursue opportunities with courage.

Growth and self-love are not abstract ideals. They are practical habits: learning how you learn, setting healthy boundaries, respecting yourself, and developing resilience through mistakes and challenges. Each stumble becomes a stepping stone, each failure a lesson in disguise. Thomas Edison famously said, *"I have not failed. I've just found 10,000 ways that won't work."* That kind of mindset comes from valuing yourself enough to persist, no matter the setbacks.

At the heart of growth is the decision to keep becoming. Growth means saying: *I am not stuck in who I was yesterday; I have the power to improve today.* It is learning to forgive yourself, celebrate your little wins, and embrace the reality that you are still a work in progress.

Self-love adds the fuel. It whispers, *"I am enough"* when comparison tempts you to feel less-than. It gives you the courage to say no to toxic friendships, to protect your time and energy, and to respect yourself as much as you respect others. Without it, growth feels like striving; with it, growth feels like transformation.

This section will walk you through the building blocks of resilience, confidence, contentment, and respect. It will remind you that mistakes do not define you, that your differences are your strength, and that valuing yourself sets the tone for how others will treat you. Growth is not a finish line but a lifelong journey—and self-love is the strength that carries you along the way.

50 Things to Help You Win

In Life, Money & Relationships

Confidence Comes from Doing, Not Just Knowing

The more you act on what you know, the more you believe in what you can do.

Think back to the first time you tried to ride a bicycle. Were you confident? Definitely not. With the tyres wobbling, your hands gripping the handlebars too tightly, your legs struggling to pedal, and your whole body trying desperately not to fall; you were anything but confident.

But after a few tries, something changed. Slowly, you got better at balancing. Your body began to remember what to do. And soon, without even thinking about it, you were riding smoothly. The fear faded, and in its place came something new; confidence. Why? Because you *knew* what you were doing, and more importantly, you *trusted yourself* to do it again. That's the real meaning of confidence: trusting yourself.

Here's the secret: there's no way to build confidence without action. You can read all the books in the world, watch tutorials, or hear advice from others but until you *try*, you won't truly feel confident. Confidence grows through doing, failing, trying again, and improving.

If you don't feel confident about something, it usually means one of two things:

1. You don't know how to do it yet.

2. You haven't practised enough.

And both can change! Confidence is not some magical gift certain people are born with. It's a skill you build, step by step, through practice. Everyone—yes, everyone—gets better with effort and experience.

So the next time you feel nervous about speaking up in class, playing in a match, or trying something new, remember this: it's not that you're not confident, it's that you're not confident *yet*. And the only way to change that is to keep showing up, keep practising, and keep trusting that every small step is moving you forward.

Confidence doesn't come overnight, but it *does* come. And when it does, it feels like flying; just like riding that bike for the very first time without falling.

Wisdom in One Line: Confidence isn't something you wait for, it's something you build by doing.

To think about...

- What's something new you want to try, even if you're nervous?
- How will practising it help your confidence grow?

In Life, Money & Relationships

Hard Work and the Extra Mile

Whatever you're doing, give it your best like you're doing it for God, not just to impress people.

These days, phrases like "soft life" are everywhere. And let's be honest, they make sense. No one is asking you to work yourself to death or carry the weight of the world on your shoulders. Life is not about endless stress or burnout. But here's the truth: there's still a powerful place for hard work and the extra mile. Together, they are the keys that open the door to excellence.

Hard work doesn't mean slaving away without joy. It means showing up with diligence and focus. It's choosing to do your assignments well, finishing the chores you start, practising until you improve, and not quitting just because something gets tough. Hard work says, *I take pride in what I do, and I want it done well.*

Then there's the extra mile; the part that makes you stand out. Anybody can do the bare minimum. Anybody can tick the boxes and scrape by. But when you go further than expected, you stand out. Going the extra mile may be as minimal as you adding a creative touch to a school project, staying behind to help clean up when no one else does, or offering a kind word when you don't have to. The extra mile is not about working yourself to exhaustion; it's about pushing yourself out of mediocre into excellence.

Think about people you admire: athletes, musicians, leaders, inventors. Behind every success story is a pattern of hard work and small decisions to do more than what was required. That's why those people stood out. And the same can be true for you. The difference between average and excellence is often the little decision to do just a little more than everyone else.

Now, let's be clear: this is not about being a workaholic. Rest, fun, and balance are essential for wholesome living, but when it's time to put in effort, don't shy away from it. See it as an opportunity to invest in yourself and your future. Anything less than your best is you selling yourself short.

So don't be afraid of hard work. Don't shy away from the extra mile. These habits build character, open opportunities, and help you become someone others can trust and respect. When you commit to giving your best, the only way from there is up.

Wisdom in One Line: Excellence comes from diligence and going beyond the required minimum.

To think about...

- When was the last time you went "the extra mile"?
- How did it feel to give more than expected?

In Life, Money & Relationships

Seek Excellence

"Excellence is doing ordinary things extraordinarily well."
– John W. Gardner

Never settle for mediocrity. It's easy to do "just enough" to get by, but mediocrity robs you of your potential and leaves you with regret. Excellence, on the other hand, unlocks doors, develops your gifts, and allows you to leave a mark that lasts.

Think about it: anything worth doing is worth doing well. Whether it's completing a homework assignment, helping at home, or serving in church, each task is an opportunity to practise diligence.

Excellence is not about perfection; it's about consistently giving your best. Over time, those small choices to give your best add up, shaping your character and preparing you for bigger opportunities.

One striking example of excellence is a man who lived in Babylon. His name was Daniel. Although he lived in Babylon, he was actually taken from his home and had to live as a foreigner in Babylon.

While there, he distinguished himself so much that the king noticed him. H was so excellent that he was preferred over all the other princes in the land and the King made him the leader of everyone. His faithfulness, discipline, and attention to detail made him stand out, even in a culture that opposed his values. His commitment to excellence earned him favour and influence.

Excellence is powerful because it does three things:

1. **It honours God.** When you give your best, you show that you value the gifts and opportunities He has placed in your life.
2. **It inspires others.** People notice when you do more than expected. Your example can encourage them to raise their own standards.
3. **It creates opportunities.** Excellence is attractive; it sets you apart in school, at work, in your relationships, and in your leadership style.

So don't just aim to be "good enough." Choose to be extraordinary. Be thorough in your schoolwork, faithful in your commitments, and intentional in your growth. Let your work speak for itself and reflect your faith and character.

Excellence is not a one-time act; it's a lifestyle. And as you seek it daily, you'll discover new opportunities, gain recognition before people who will open up big doors for you that you never imagined.

Wisdom in One Line: What is worth doing is worth doing well.

To think about...

- What's one small area where you could give your best today?
- How does excellence differ from perfection?

50 Things to Help You Win

Integrity, Honesty, and Character Matter

"The time is always right to do what is right."
– Martin Luther King Jr.

Life will bring you countless choices: some easy, others hard. And in many of those moments, you'll face a decision between doing what's right and taking the easy way out. Choosing honesty, integrity, and strong character may not always feel convenient, but they are the foundations on which you can build a life; a life you can be proud of.

Honesty means telling the truth, even when it's uncomfortable. Maybe you're tempted to cover up a mistake, cheat on a test, or tell a *small* lie to avoid getting into trouble. It might feel like the easy way out in the moment, but lies have a way of trapping you. One lie often leads to another, and before long, if you're not careful, you'll find yourself entangled in a web of lies you spun on yourself.

The truth, on the other hand, may sting for a moment, but it builds freedom and trust that last much longer. People might forget your words, but they'll always remember if you are a trustworthy person.

Integrity is about being consistent; doing the right thing even when no one is watching. It's like having an invisible compass that points you toward what's right. Your integrity shows when you resist peer pressure, keep your promises, and act in line with your values. It's not about being perfect, but about being real and dependable.

Character is who you are at your core. It's built day by day through the little choices you make: how you treat people, how you handle mistakes, and how you respond under pressure. A strong character means others can trust and respect you. And here's the amazing part: when you live with character, you don't just earn the respect of others, you also gain confidence in yourself, because you know you're living true to who you are.

Living with honesty, integrity, and character may not always make you popular. In fact, sometimes it will cost you. But in the long run, it will set you apart in the best possible way. Teachers, friends, coaches, and even future employers will notice that you're someone they can rely on. More importantly, you will notice! You will carry the peace of knowing you don't have to hide or pretend.

So the next time you're tempted to lie, cheat, or cut corners, pause and ask yourself: *Will this build my character or break it?* Because at the end of the day, what matters most isn't how popular you are or how good you look on the outside, it's the kind of person you're becoming on the inside.

Wisdom in One Line: Always choose truth, integrity, and character, because who you are matters more than anything you have.

To think about...

- What would your friends say about your character?
- When was the last time you chose honesty even though it was hard?

50 Things to Help You Win

In Life, Money & Relationships

It's OK To Make Mistakes

"Anyone who has never made a mistake has never tried anything new."
– Albert Einstein

As you go through life, you will make choices; some good, some not so great. Sometimes, you will make decisions that don't turn out the way you expected. That's completely normal! What truly matters is what you do next.

Whenever you make a mistake, the initial response is usually to feel bad and hide in shame, but you should never let your mistakes define you. So instead of feeling bad and ashamed the next time you make a mistake, ask yourself these two important questions:

1. **What did I learn?** – Every mistake teaches you something. Maybe you learned to be more careful, to listen more, or to think things through before acting. Mistakes can be great teachers if you are willing to learn from them.

2. **What will I do better next time?** – Once you understand what went wrong, you can make better choices in the future. This helps you grow and improve, making you wiser and stronger.

Think of mistakes as stepping stones, not roadblocks. They are just part of the journey, helping to build a stronger, wiser, and more capable version of you. Never allow yourself to be trapped in self-pity—it's a dangerous place to stay. Feeling bad for too long can make you doubt yourself, and that is not what God wants for you.

Instead of focusing on failure, focus on learning. Instead of giving up, try again. Every successful person you admire has made mistakes too, but they didn't let those mistakes stop them. Neither should you!

Remember: You are more than your mistakes. Keep moving forward, growing, and trusting God to help you become the best version of yourself.

Wisdom in One Line: Mistakes are lessons that make you wiser.

To think about...

- What's a mistake that taught you something valuable?
- How can you remind yourself that mistakes don't define you?

In Life, Money & Relationships

Life's Twists and Turns: Stay Flexible

"Every adversity, every failure, every heartbreak, carries with it the seed of an equal or greater benefit."
– Napoleon Hill

Life doesn't always follow the script you imagine. You might set goals, dream big dreams, or create a plan that feels perfect, and then *boom!* something unexpected happens. Maybe you don't make the sports team you trained for, your best friend suddenly moves away, or your carefully thought-out plans fall apart in a single moment. It's frustrating, even discouraging. But here's the truth: life isn't working against you, it's working for you.

Thousands of years ago, there was a young man named Joseph. He loved to dream and had amazing dreams about his future, but his path was anything but smooth. He was betrayed by his own brothers, sold into slavery, and even thrown into prison for something he didn't do. From the outside, it looked like his life was falling apart. But all those twists and setbacks were shaping him for something greater. In the end, he rose to become a ruler in Egypt and saved an entire nation from famine. What looked like detours were really stepping stones divinely orchestrated by God.

It's the same with you. Go ahead: dream big, set goals, and work hard. But when life throws you a curveball *and it will*, don't let it knock you down for good. Stay flexible. Learn from the challenge. Sometimes what feels like a setback is simply preparation for the next stage of your journey.

If you fail a test, lose an opportunity, or face disappointment, don't let it define your worth. Take a deep breath. Ask yourself what you can learn from it. Then keep moving forward. Even when things don't go according to plan, God is still guiding you toward something amazing.

Remember, the road to your future won't always be straight. There will be bends, bumps, and detours. But every twist and turn is shaping you into someone stronger, wiser, and more ready for the greatness ahead.

So don't fear life's surprises rather embrace them. Trust the process. Flexibility is strength, and when you stay open to learning, you'll discover that even the hardest detours can lead to your greatest destination.

Wisdom in One Line: Flexibility turns setbacks into stepping stones.

To think about...

- What's a plan you had that didn't work out?
- What did you learn from the change in direction?

In Life, Money & Relationships

There Is Always a Way Out

"If you run into a wall, don't turn around and give up. Figure out how to climb it."
— *Michael Jordan*

Life will throw challenges at you. Sometimes it feels like doors slam shut, opportunities slip away, or problems pile up so high that you can't see past them. In those moments, it's easy to believe you're stuck with no way forward. But here's the truth: there is *always* a way out. The fact that you can't see the solution right now doesn't mean it doesn't exist; it might just be hidden, waiting for you to discover it.

Often, your ability to find solutions depends on what you know. The more you grow in wisdom, knowledge, and experience, the clearer the path becomes. That's why learning, asking questions, and seeking advice are important tools for living a wholesome life. Making use of them equips you to navigate obstacles when they appear.

So what can you do when you feel stuck and don't know what to do?

1. **Pray and ask God for guidance.** He sees what you don't and knows exactly where the answer is. Trust Him to lead you in the right direction.
2. **Ask for help.** Talk to someone wiser than you: a parent, teacher, mentor, or pastor. They may have walked the same road before

and can give you advice that saves you time and stress.
3. **Learn more.** Read, research, and ask questions. Sometimes the answer is simply knowledge you haven't gained yet.
4. **Stay calm and think it through.** Panic magnifies problems. Take a deep breath, slow down, and allow yourself space to think clearly.

The key is to never give up too quickly. The solution might not appear in the way you expect, but it's always there. Keep growing. Keep seeking. Keep trusting God.

You are never truly stuck. With patience, wisdom, and faith, you will always find the way forward.

Wisdom in One Line: Every challenge carries the seed of a solution.

To think about...

- What do you usually do when you feel stuck?
- Who could you go to for advice the next time you face a tough situation?

In Life, Money & Relationships

Decide to Decide Well

"It is in your moments of decision that your destiny is shaped."
– Tony Robbins

Did you know that every decision you make whether big or small, has the power to shape your life? It's true! Think about it: the decision to brush your teeth means your friends won't avoid you because of bad breath. The decision to get out of bed on time gives you an extra hour in your day. And what could you do with that hour? You could read, learn a new skill, work on a hobby, or even relax and enjoy a little peace.

At first, these choices might seem small or unimportant. But here's the secret: small decisions stack up, like bricks in a tower. The more you make better decisions, the taller and stronger your tower becomes; and that tower is your future.

Every time you make a wise choice; you're building something valuable. Choosing to study instead of spending the whole evening gaming could mean better grades, which could lead to better opportunities. Choosing to be kind instead of ignoring someone could spark a meaningful friendship. Even little things like finishing your homework today instead of procrastinating add up to big results over time.

Of course, no one makes perfect choices all the time. You'll make mistakes, just like everyone else.

But mistakes don't define you; they teach you. A bad decision is just a chance to learn how to make a better one next time. What matters most is that you don't give up. Keep choosing, keep growing, and keep building.

Next time you're faced with a choice, big or small, pause for a moment and remember: your decision is powerful. Use it wisely. Decide to decide well. Because the future you're dreaming of is built on the decisions you make today.

Wisdom in One Line: Your decisions today create your future tomorrow.

To think about...

- What's a small decision you made recently? Did it help or hurt your day?
- How can you practise pausing before you decide?

In Life, Money & Relationships

Practice Diligence

"Diligence is the mother of good luck."
– Benjamin Franklin

Abiye loved football. Every day after school, he would rush to the field, practising his dribbles and shots long after his teammates had gone home. But despite his effort, he wasn't the best player on his team. In fact, some of the other boys laughed at his mistakes.

"Why do you even bother, Abiye?" one of them teased after he missed an easy goal during practice. "You're never going to be as good as David."

David was the star of the team: fast, skilled, and always scoring goals. But Abiye didn't let the comparison discourage him. He knew he wasn't racing against David; he was racing against himself. His goal wasn't to be the best instantly but to be better than he was yesterday. So while others relaxed after training, Abiye stayed back, working on his weak foot, practising penalties, and building his stamina.

Weeks later, the team reached the finals of the local tournament. Everyone expected David to carry them to victory. But just before halftime, disaster struck; David twisted his ankle and had to leave the game. The score was 1–1, and with only minutes left, the team desperately needed someone to step up.

Abiye remembered all those extra hours he had put in when no one was watching. When the ball came to him, he didn't hesitate. With focus and power, he struck it into the top corner and GOAL! The crowd erupted. His teammates lifted him high, and his coach smiled with pride.

That day, Abiye discovered something powerful: talent is a gift, but diligence is what turns potential into success. Hard work may not get attention right away, but over time it builds strength, confidence, and readiness for the moment that counts.

Success doesn't come to those who wait; it comes to those who *work*. And diligence; steady, consistent effort, is what sets apart those who shine when it matters most.

Wisdom in One Line: Consistency and effort outweigh natural talent.

To think about...

- Where in your life could you be more consistent right now?
- How can diligence make you more prepared for opportunities?

In Life, Money & Relationships

Be Restless

"Stay hungry, stay foolish."
– Steve Jobs

Have you ever felt that little wiggle inside you, that voice that whispers, *"I can do better"* or *"There's more out there for me"*? That feeling is called restlessness. It's not a bad thing. In fact, it's one of the best motivators you'll ever have. Restlessness is like your inner explorer, always curious, always searching, always pushing you to grow.

Think about a bird learning to fly. The first few attempts are clumsy. The bird stumbles, wobbles, maybe even falls. But does it quit? No! It keeps flapping, trying again and again until it soars. That's what restlessness feels like; it's the desire to try harder, to improve, and to rise above where you are now.

You've probably felt it in your favourite game. Maybe you want to level up, score more points, or learn a new move. That drive to get better, to practise until you nail it, is restlessness at work. And it doesn't just apply to games; it shows up in school, hobbies, sports, friendships, and even your relationship with God.

Here's the key: restlessness isn't about being unhappy with yourself or thinking you're not good enough. It's about having a spirit of adventure, a hunger to explore, and a desire to see how much more you can become. It's about curiosity—the willingness to ask questions, learn new things, and step outside your comfort zone.

When you feel restless, don't push it away. Embrace it! Use it as fuel to chase a new challenge, try a new skill, or set a bigger goal. That little wiggle inside you is pointing toward your potential.

Remember, the best things in life often begin with restlessness; the quiet spark that tells you not to settle, but to keep learning, keep growing, and keep reaching higher.

Wisdom in One Line: A holy discontent fuels growth and discovery.

To think about...

- What area of your life makes you feel like, "I can do better"?
- How could you channel that restlessness into growth?

In Life, Money & Relationships

Flip the Switch: Choosing Gratitude

"Gratitude turns what we have into enough."
– Aesop

Have you ever noticed how sometimes it feels like the whole world is filled with sad news? It's easy to get caught up in everything that's wrong and forget about all the amazing things that are right. It's like when the sky is cloudy, we forget that the sun is still shining brightly behind those clouds.

Imagine a lightbulb. It's there, ready to brighten a room, but if you don't turn on the light, the room stays dark. You could be surrounded by lightbulbs, but without turning them on, it's still gloomy. Happiness works the same way. We all have so many wonderful things in our lives: our families, our friends, our pets, our favourite books, the warmth of the sun on our skin, or even a delicious meal, but sometimes we barely notice them because we are so used to having them present.

This is why it is so important to practise gratitude. Gratitude means being thankful for all the good things in your life, big or small. It is acknowledging the blessings around you. This is not you pretending that bad things don't exist; it's you making the decision to be grateful for the good instead of focusing on the bad.

Why not try a little "Thanksgiving Time" every day? It doesn't have to be complicated. Just take five minutes to stop and think about the things you're grateful for. You could even write them down in *Gratitude Journal*. You can write about the friend who made you laugh, the pet that curled up beside you, or the sunset that painted the sky. It could even be something as simple but important as the roof over your head or the food on your plate.

This might feel awkward in the beginning and you may have to do a deep soul search to see what you're grateful for, but it is a rewarding adventure. The more you do it, the easier it gets. And soon, you'll notice how different it makes you feel.

Flip that gratitude switch! Celebrate the good things in your life and watch how much brighter your world becomes.

Wisdom in One Line: Gratitude lights up even the darkest days.

To think about...

- What are three things you're grateful for today?
- How does gratitude change the way you see challenges?

In Life, Money & Relationships

Listen More

"We have two ears and one mouth so that we can listen twice as much as we speak."
– Epictetus

We all have so much to say, with so many thoughts longing to spill out. There's nothing wrong with that. Learning to speak up and share your opinions is an important life skill to learn. However, learning to listen at least twice as much as you speak makes one very wise.

Why? Because listening is the gateway to wisdom. You learn from what others have been through. Your parents, teachers, friends, and even strangers have experiences that can help you navigate life better. When you truly listen, you gain insights that could save you from making mistakes or help you see the world in a new way.

Imagine this: Hamid and Daniel both love football. Hamid listens carefully when his coach corrects his mistakes, while Daniel ignores advice and insists on doing things his way. Over time, Hamid improves on his errors, while Daniel keeps repeating the same mistakes over and over again. By the end of the season, Hamid had become one of the best players on their team, while Daniel was struggling to keep up. The difference? One listened, and the other didn't.

Listening doesn't mean just hearing words; it means paying attention, asking questions, and thinking about what is being said. It means being open to learning, even when you don't agree. It also shows respect and makes people more willing to listen to you in return.

When you're in a conversation, pause. Instead of just waiting for your turn to talk, really listen. You might be surprised by how much you learn!

Wisdom in One Line: Wisdom grows in the soil of listening ears.

To think about...

- Do you listen more, or do you talk more?
- Who could you practise really listening to this week?

Resilience keeps you standing, but purpose shows you where to walk. Once you've learned to value yourself, embrace growth, and practise gratitude, you are ready to aim higher, to pursue excellence, and to live with intention. In the next part, you'll see how purpose and discipline transform ordinary effort into extraordinary impact.

50 Things to Help You Win

Part Five: Living with Purpose and Pursuing Excellence

"We are what we repeatedly do. Excellence then, is not an act, but a habit."
– Aristotle

If self-love builds the foundation, purpose and excellence form the structure of a life well-lived. Purpose gives direction, while excellence determines how far that direction takes you. Studies show that people with a strong sense of purpose live up to seven years longer on average, with lower stress and greater satisfaction in their work and relationships (Journal of Positive Psychology, 2019). Purpose does more than inspire—it anchors you when life's storms threaten to derail your course.

Excellence, on the other hand, is not perfection. It is the daily habit of doing your best, even in small things. Daniel, in ancient history, was described as someone who had "an excellent spirit", and that distinction opened doors of influence in one of history's greatest empires. Excellence isn't about being flawless; it's about being faithful—faithful to your values, your responsibilities, and the vision God has placed in your heart.

Purpose and excellence should go hand in hand. Your purpose defines *why you are here*; your excellence defines *how the world will experience you*. Together, they transform ordinary effort into extraordinary impact. Think of athletes who train relentlessly not only to win medals but also to inspire generations. Or innovators like the Wright brothers, who imagined flight before it was possible and then committed themselves to tireless, excellent work until the dream became reality.

In Life, Money & Relationships

This section will guide you through lessons on diligence, vision, leadership, and integrity. It will show you how to embrace opportunities, stay anchored when challenges come, and cultivate habits that set you apart. Excellence is not achieved in a single moment of brilliance but in the steady rhythm of consistent effort. Purpose ensures that rhythm is not wasted on the wrong song.

By combining the clarity of purpose with the discipline of excellence, you move from mere survival to meaningful living. You stop chasing applause and start creating impact. You stop competing with others and start running your own race. And in the process, you discover the deep fulfilment of a life lived with intention and mastery.

50 Things to Help You Win

In Life, Money & Relationships

Learn How You *Learn* and Never Be Afraid to Aim High

"Shoot for the moon. Even if you miss, you'll land among the stars."
– Norman Vincent Peale

When I was in primary school, everything came easily to me. I hardly ever studied, yet I scored top marks. But when I moved on to secondary school, everything changed. Suddenly, I had to juggle 14 or 15 different subjects, each with its own assignments and tests, and I found myself struggling academically for the first time. The ease I once took for granted was gone, and I began to struggle.

Then, in what I can only describe as an answer to prayer, I stumbled upon a book; its title and author long forgotten, but its lessons etched into my life forever. That little book taught me two principles that became my secret weapons for success: learn how *you* learn; and never be afraid to aim high.

The first principle was revolutionary for me. The book suggested creating rhymes to memorise facts, isolating myself to read aloud, and repeating lessons in my own words. At the time, I didn't realise this was because I had an auditory learning style. All I knew was that, suddenly, studying felt possible again. For the first time, I understood that learning is not a "one size fits all."

Each of us has a unique way our brains absorb and process information. Some learn best by listening, others by writing things down, drawing diagrams, or even practising hands-on. Discovering your learning style is like finding the right key for a lock—it opens the door to understanding and mastery.

The second principle was just as powerful: *Aim high*. The book paraphrased it as, "Aim for the moon, and even if you miss, you'll land among the stars." That phrase burned itself into my mind. I realised that there was no shame in stretching myself toward lofty goals, even if I didn't hit them perfectly every time. Setting high standards pushed me to grow, to reach beyond my comfort zone, and to pursue excellence with courage.

Looking back, these two principles—knowing how I learn and aiming high—have shaped everything I've done since. They turned moments of fear into opportunities for growth, and they gave me tools to succeed not just in school, but in life.

Here's the truth: life will often present challenges that seem bigger than you. But if you take time to understand how you learn best and refuse to settle for mediocrity, you will always find a way through.

Don't be afraid to experiment with study techniques, reflection methods, or creative approaches until you discover what works for you. And when you do, set your sights high.

In Life, Money & Relationships

Even if you don't always reach the *moon*, you'll find yourself further than you ever imagined, among the stars.

Wisdom in One Line: Understanding how you learn unlocks your potential.

To think about...

- What study method works best for you: reading, listening, or hands-on practical?
- What's one high goal you'd like to aim for this year?

50 Things to Help You Win

In Life, Money & Relationships

Follow Your Interests

"The place God calls you to is the place where your deep gladness and the world's deep hunger meet."
– Frederick Buechner

Do you remember the story or perhaps the movie of *Alice in Wonderland*? Alice followed a rabbit that caught her attention and, before she knew it, tumbled into a whole new world.

That's what happens when you pay attention to the things that spark your curiosity. Interests are not random distractions; they are often clues pointing you toward your future, carefully placed there by your Creator.

Your job is simple but important: take notice of what fascinates you and follow it. Maybe you love solving puzzles, telling stories, sketching, building things, or helping people. Those passions are like breadcrumbs on the path toward your purpose. They're not accidents; they are signposts.

So, how do you follow your interests? Start by learning more about it. In today's world, information is literally at your fingertips. Instead of losing endless hours to entertainment: scrolling through social media, binge-watching shows, or playing games, use your time to explore your passions.

Watch educational YouTube videos, read books and articles, listen to podcasts, and even use tools like ChatGPT to expand your knowledge. Every bit of learning moves you closer to mastery.

The more you nurture your interests, the more they grow into skills. And skills have value. One day, what started as a simple curiosity could become the very thing that opens doors, creates opportunities, or even earns you a living. Imagine the joy of not only doing what you love but also being rewarded for it. Work becomes less of a burden and more of a calling when it aligns with your passion.

This is why following your interests is so important. It's not just about having fun; it's about uncovering who you are, what you're good at, and what God may be leading you to do with your life. When you give attention to the things that make you come alive, you're not just entertaining yourself; you're preparing for your future.

So go ahead. Pay attention to the *rabbit holes* of curiosity in your life. Explore them. Learn from them. Grow through them. What better way to live than by doing what you truly love and discovering along the way that those *loves* were planted in you for a reason?

Wisdom in One Line: Your passions point you toward your purpose.

To think about...

- What's one interest you'd like to explore further?
- How could that interest connect to your future purpose?

50 Things to Help You Win

In Life, Money & Relationships

See Before You *See*

"The future belongs to those who see possibilities before they become obvious."
– John Sculley

It costs nothing to imagine. In fact, imagination is one of the greatest gifts we've been given as human beings by God. It enables us to envision something before it happens—to picture it in our minds before it becomes reality. These mental pictures are powerful because they spark passion, stir motivation, and drive us to turn visions into real achievements.

Every great invention, every breakthrough, started as an idea in someone's imagination. The Wright brothers saw the possibility of flying before airplanes existed. Thomas Edison imagined electric lights before the world moved beyond candles. Martin Luther King Jr. envisioned a future of racial equality long before it became a global movement. To others, their ideas seemed invisible, even impossible. But because they dared to see first, their visions became real.

There's a saying: *"You can't be what you can't see."* It's true that having role models can inspire us, showing us what's possible. But what if you're the first in your family, your school, or even your generation to dream of something? Even without examples to follow, the vision in your mind can become the seed for your future. Once you can see it, you can begin the journey toward achieving it.

Still, imagination alone is not enough. Dreams without action remain just *dreams*. The real test of your belief in a vision is what you're willing to do about it. Hard work, consistency, learning, and persistence are what transform invisible ideas into visible results. It's your effort that brings your imagination to life.

The truth is, the world we live in today has been shaped by people who dared to see before they *saw*. They didn't wait for permission. They didn't wait for everyone else to understand. They trusted their vision, worked hard, and changed history.

What about you? What dreams have you been carrying? Will you choose to see them in your heart before they appear in your hands? What actions will you take to bring them alive?

Wisdom in One Line: Everything great begins as a vision, so see it before you *see* it.

To think about...

- What's one dream that feels so real in your imagination, though it hasn't happened yet?
- What step could you take to move that dream closer to reality?

In Life, Money & Relationships

The Dreams You Conceive Now Can Be Your Future

"Everything you can imagine is real."
– Pablo Picasso

When I was 11, I baked my first fruit cake. My mum got someone to help me, but he left before we even got started. So my siblings and I were left on our own. Guess how it turned out? Well, not so great; but that experience sparked something in me.

A few years later, fresh out of secondary school, I tried baking again. I didn't have a recipe, no measurements, not even a measuring cup. I simply went to the market, gathered the ingredients, got home, and baked. To my surprise, everyone loved it! That was when I began to dream of starting a bakery business.

With my makeshift oven (sand in a pot), I practised whenever I could. By the time I got to the university, I was already known amongst my friends as a baker. Years later, that childhood dream has become a reality: today I run a thriving catering and confectionery business in two countries.

Here's the lesson: you are never too young to dream. This is the best time to picture your future. Dreams may start small: a thought, an idea, a hobby, but with practice, persistence, and the guidance of the Holy Spirit, they can grow into a reality that shapes your life.

Dare to dream. Write them down. Pray over them. Let God breathe on them. Your dreams are seeds of your future.

Wisdom in One Line: The dreams you hold today can become the reality you live tomorrow.

To think about...

- Write down any dream you have, no matter how little it seems.
- Take five minutes out each day to imagine what could happen if that dream comes true.

In Life, Money & Relationships

Everyone's Journey Is Different

"Don't compare your chapter one to someone else's chapter twenty."
– Unknown

No two people's journeys are the same. Try and imagine life as a treasure hunt; not one where you borrow someone else's map, but one where you've been given a unique path to follow. This path is supposed to lead you to discover the biggest treasure of your life—yourself!

Every experience you have: the things you love, the things that frustrate you, and even the challenges you face are like clues leading you closer to the treasure of discovering your true purpose.

Take Lu Ming Hao, for example. He loved fixing things, whether they were broken toys or his sister's bicycle. He would spend hours figuring out how they worked, and he wouldn't give up until he had fixed the problem. However Lu Ming Hao struggled with writing essays in school unlike his best friend Sam who could write stories effortlessly. Lu Ming Hao wished he could be more like Sam in that area.

One day, his teacher noticed how quickly Lu Ming Hao repaired a broken classroom fan. "You're really good at this!" she said to him. That small moment opened Lu Ming Hao's eyes. What if his love for fixing things wasn't random? What if it was a clue to his purpose?

So instead of wishing he was more like Sam, Lu Ming Hao started paying attention to his own gifts. He watched engineering videos online, joined a robotics club, and discovered he had real talent for designing and building. The thing he once overlooked turned out to be the very thing that set him apart.

Here's the truth: your greatest success won't come from copying someone else's journey; it will come from following your own. God placed unique treasures inside you—your passions, your gifts, your curiosities, and yes, even your struggles. All of them are part of the map that leads to your future.

So, stop wishing you were someone else. Don't waste energy comparing your life to theirs. Instead, pay attention to what excites you, what challenges you, and what makes you come alive. Study your journey. Learn from your experiences. And trust that you are exactly where you need to be to discover the greatness inside you.

Your path may look different from everyone else's but that's the point. Your own path will lead you to your purpose.

Wisdom in One Line: Your gifts and experiences shape your destiny.

To think about...

- What activity makes you lose track of time because you love it so much?
- How could that be a clue to your purpose?

50 Things to Help You Win

In Life, Money & Relationships

Run Your Own Race

"Comparison is the thief of joy."
– Theodore Roosevelt

Life can feel like a race, but here's the truth: you're not racing against anyone else. You have your own path, your own pace, and your own finish line. Sometimes, you'll find friends, classmates, or teammates running beside you, cheering you on. Other times, it may feel like you're running alone. And that's okay because your race is yours alone to run.

It's good to challenge yourself and aim higher. A little healthy competition can push you to grow and bring out your best but when competition turns into comparison, it becomes dangerous. Comparison shifts your focus from growth to jealousy, from progress to pressure.

Take school exams as an example. They're designed to test what you've learned, but in some schools, students are ranked by position. Suddenly, it's no longer about testing understanding, it's about who is *number one*. This can make students feel like their value depends on outperforming others. Some may even feel pressured to cheat just to stay ahead, while others get discouraged or angry when someone else scores higher. That's not healthy growth; it's unhealthy competition.

But here's what you need to remember: you're not meant to compete with anyone else. You're meant to compete with yourself. The only record you need to break is your own.

So instead of asking, *"Am I better than them?"* start asking, *"Am I better than I was yesterday?"* Did I learn something new today? Did I practise a skill longer than I did yesterday? Did I choose kindness, even when it was hard? Those small wins add up, and over time, they'll carry you far.

And don't forget: God has set the pace for your life. He knows the route, the hurdles, and the finish line designed for you. No one else can run your race the way you can. So stay in your lane. Focus on your progress. Celebrate your growth. And keep running with your eyes fixed forward, not sideways.

Run your race with patience, with faith, and with determination. Because the best race you can ever run is the one that takes you closer to the person God created you to be.

Wisdom in One Line: Compete only with who you were yesterday.

To think about...

- When do you find yourself comparing to others most often?
- What's one way you can measure yourself by your own progress instead?

Opportunities Lead to Opportunities

"Success is the sum of small efforts, repeated day in and day out."
– Robert Collier

Many years ago, I attended a church service where the preacher said something that stuck with me: *"Opportunities lead to opportunities."* At first, it sounded simple, almost obvious. But the more I thought about it, the more powerful it became. That phrase imprinted itself on my heart, and I hope, after reading this, it will be imprinted on yours too.

What does it mean? Quite simply, opportunities create momentum. When you take one opportunity and do it well, it sets things in motion and often creates space for new ones. Saying yes whether to a job, a project, or even a small responsibility builds a kind of forward motion that opens doors you didn't expect. Opportunities have a way of multiplying, but only if you recognise them and act on them.

Here's the challenge: momentum is often lost because we overlook the small beginnings. We imagine that opportunities will always be big, shiny, impossible-to-miss moments. But often, they come disguised as something ordinary, inconvenient, or even challenging tasks.

The Cambridge Dictionary defines an opportunity as *"a situation in which it is possible for you to do something, or a possibility of doing something."* Notice that it's not just about what comes to you, it's also about what you initiate. Momentum doesn't build itself. Opportunities are created by the choices you make, the effort you put in, and the way you show up in everyday situations.

For example, when I was in secondary school, I underperformed academically. But at university, I decided to build momentum by doing things differently. I studied daily in the library, worked harder, and treated every day as a chance to improve. That consistent effort created an opportunity: I graduated first in my class and was accepted directly into a PhD program without having to complete a master's degree; something unusual in my field. One opportunity, fuelled by momentum, opened the way for another.

That's the way life works. One door leads to the next, but only if you keep moving. What looks like a "small" opportunity today: a school project, a part-time job, volunteering to help, speaking up in class, might generate the momentum for bigger things tomorrow. The size of the opportunity is not what matters; what matters is how you treat it and whether you keep going.

It's said that beauty is in the eye of the beholder. I believe opportunities are the same. If you train your eyes to notice them, and your heart to act on them, you will build momentum over time that will propel you forward and make you more equipped to seize more opportunities as they come.

Wisdom in One Line: Opportunities multiply when you recognise them and you build momentum by acting on them.

To think about...

- What small opportunity is in front of you right now?
- How could saying *yes* now lead to bigger doors later?

50 Things to Help You Win

In Life, Money & Relationships

Make Hay While the Sun Shines

"For everything there is a season, and a time for every matter under heaven."
– The Teacher

One day, I was speaking to my mother when she said something that stayed with me: *"It's good to make hay while the sun shines."* At first, it sounded like just another saying, but its wisdom has echoed in my mind ever since.

On the surface, it's a farming phrase. Farmers can only dry hay properly when the weather is good. If they delay, the rain may come, and the chance is lost. But this is more than farming advice, it's a life principle: act while the time is right.

Opportunities are tied to timing. Conditions change. What feels easy today might be twice as hard tomorrow. That's why procrastination is so dangerous—it assumes the same window will stay open, when in fact, it may close forever.

Think about education. While you can return to school at any age which is admirable, the experience is not the same at every stage. A 17-year-old fresh out of secondary school has fewer responsibilities and will adapt more quickly to university life than a parent in their 40s juggling children, bills, and work. The opportunity still exists truly, but now it comes with more weight and sacrifice.

Every season of life carries its own opportunities: childhood for laying foundations, teenage years for discovery, young adulthood for building and preparation. If you miss certain opportunities in their time, you may still grasp them later, but not without extra effort and sometimes not at all.

That's why timing matters. Life is not just about recognising opportunities; it's about recognising them early, *when they matter most*. Seizing the moment creates momentum for the next. Missing it can mean years of delay or complete denial in extreme cases.

Here's the truth: don't wait for a "perfect time." The perfect time is usually now. If you have the chance to learn, grow, serve, or step into something meaningful; do it while the sun is shining.

Wisdom in One Line: Seize opportunities when they arise, because they may not come again.

To think about...

- What opportunity is available to you right now that might not last forever?
- How can you act on it today?

Purpose and excellence can take you far, but without an anchor, even the strongest can drift. The storms of life are real, and achievement alone won't hold you steady. That's why the final foundation must be laid: anchoring yourself in God. He is the unchanging centre that keeps everything else secure—your identity, your relationships, your resilience, and your purpose.

50 Things to Help You Win

Part Six: Anchored in God

"We have this hope as an anchor for the soul, firm and secure."

– The Holy Bible

Life is full of changes. Grades rise and fall, friendships shift, opportunities come and go, and even our own emotions can feel like a storm. If we try to build our identity or security on those shifting sands, we will always feel uncertain and unsteady. That's why we need something—no, Someone—unchanging to hold us firm.

Being anchored in God means rooting your life in the One who never changes, never fails, and never stops loving you. Just like a ship depends on its anchor to stay steady through the fiercest waves, we too need God to keep us grounded when life feels overwhelming. Success, popularity, and even personal strength can only carry us so far, but God's love and truth are a foundation that will not move.

In this part, you'll discover lessons that remind you who you really are—not defined by achievements or mistakes, but by God's unchanging love. You'll be encouraged to put Him first, to rely on His strength, to live with integrity, and to choose friends and values that keep you steady.

Storms will come, but with God as your anchor, you won't just survive them; you'll grow stronger, wiser, and more confident in who He has called you to be.

In Life, Money & Relationships

Put God First

"When God is at the centre of your life, everything else finds its proper place."
- Unknown

As you go through life, you'll meet people who say that God doesn't exist. Please don't believe them. You'll also meet others who admit God is real but will try to convince you to take Him casually, to treat your faith like an afterthought. Avoid this group even more. There is nothing casual about God or the relationship you should have with Him. Take God seriously.

Putting God first means recognising that He is the foundation of your life. It means paying attention to what He wants you to do and trusting that His plan for you is good. You're not here by accident. God sent you into the world through your parents for a specific purpose. If you're not sure what that purpose is, ask Him. He will show you.

When difficulties come—and they will—the first place to look for answers is God. Don't hesitate to go to Him, because He knows everything and has the solution to everything. Never doubt His ability to bring you through any trouble. And yes, it's even better when you follow Him closely and avoid unnecessary trouble in the first place.

Some people may try to tell you that believing in God is "old-fashioned." Don't fall for that lie. God never goes out of style or fashion. He is the same yesterday, today, and forever. He is good to everyone who chooses to hold on to Him, and He never lets anyone down.

Of course, life won't always look like you expect. There will be times when things happen that make you wonder, *Does God even care?* But He does—oh, He cares more than you can imagine. He loves you deeply and is working everything out perfectly, even when you can't see the full picture. Sometimes, the challenges you face are part of shaping you into the best version of yourself.

So fix this truth firmly in your heart: God loves you, and He will never plan anything bad for you. When it feels like life is falling apart, trust that He has a bigger plan unfolding.

Make it a habit to put God first in everything. When you wake up each morning, think about Him and thank Him. When you start something new, invite Him into it. Don't make big decisions—or even small ones—without seeking His guidance.

When you put God first, you'll find that your life has more clarity, more wisdom, and more purpose. You'll make fewer mistakes, and even when you stumble, you'll know He's right there to guide you back on the right track.

Wisdom in One Line: Trust that God has a perfect plan for your life and put Him first in all you do.

To think about...

- What's one area of your life where you need to put God first?
- How can you start your day with Him tomorrow?

50 Things to Help You Win

In Life, Money & Relationships

Anchored in God

If you put your trust in God, you'll be strong and steady like a mountain that can't be moved.

Jaden was used to being the smartest one in the room. His top grades made him feel important, and he loved hearing people say, *"Wow, you're so smart!"* It gave him a sense of identity. But everything changed the day he failed a big math test. His friends looked surprised, his teacher seemed disappointed, and inside, Jaden felt crushed.

That evening, he sat on his bed, staring at the red marks on his paper. *If I'm not the best, then who am I?* he thought. His grandmother walked in and noticed his downcast face. "Rough day?" she asked gently.

Jaden nodded. "I messed up. I failed. I feel... lost."

She sat beside him and smiled softly. "Jaden, do you know what happens to a tree with weak roots when a storm comes?"

He shrugged. "It falls?"

"Exactly. But a tree with deep roots? It stands firm, no matter how fierce the wind blows." She placed a hand on his shoulder. "When you build your confidence on things like grades, achievements, or what people think of you, it's like having weak roots. The moment those things change, you feel shaken. But when your confidence is in God—the One who made you, loves you, and never changes—you become unshakable."

Jaden's eyes widened a little. "So...even if I fail, I'm still me?"

His grandmother nodded. "More than that; you're still deeply loved by God. He saw you, knew you, and loved you before you ever took your first breath. His love isn't based on what you do, it's based on who He is."

Jaden smiled faintly, hope flickering in his heart. Maybe he didn't have to be perfect to matter.

The truth is, life will always change. Grades, opinions, achievements, and even friendships can shift like the wind. But God? He remains the same. His love for you doesn't rise and fall with your performance. When you root your confidence in Him, you stand firm no matter what storms come.

So, build your identity not on temporary things, but on the eternal truth of God's love. That's the anchor that will keep you steady through every season of life.

Wisdom in One Line: Your roots in God make you unshakable.

In Life, Money & Relationships

To think about...

- What do you usually base your confidence on: grades, friends, or God?
- How could trusting God more make you stronger inside?

50 Things to Help You Win

In Life, Money & Relationships

I Can Do All Things Through Christ Who Strengthens Me

When you add Christ into the equation, things that seem so hard suddenly become possible.

Life sometimes doesn't always play fair. Some days feel like a breeze; you ace your test, laugh with friends, and everything just clicks. But other days? Not so much. You feel weighed down by pressure, worried about failing, or even convinced you're not good enough. It can be overwhelming, and in those moments, it's easy to wonder if you've really got what it takes.

Here's the good news: you don't have to do life in your own strength. You were never meant to. In the Bible, it says that **when we allow Christ to give us strength, then we're able to do anything we need to do.** That is a powerful promise. It means that no matter what comes your way, you're not alone. God Himself is ready to give you the strength, courage, and wisdom you need to keep going.

Think about it: when you're facing a tough exam, trying to make the right decision, or standing up for what you believe in—even when it feels scary—you don't have to depend only on your own abilities. Christ steps in and gives you a strength that goes beyond what you could ever muster on your own.

Now, does that mean everything will suddenly become easy? Definitely not. There will still be challenges. You'll still have days when you feel tired, discouraged, or tempted to give up. But leaning on Christ changes the game. He lifts you up when you're weak, gives you peace when you're anxious, and reminds you that your worth isn't measured by your performance, but by His love.

So next time you feel like you can't do it, remember this truth: you *can*. Not because you're perfect or superhuman, but because Christ is with you. And with Him, there really are no limits. You can do all things—not some, not most—*all things* through Christ who strengthens you.

Wisdom in One Line: Christ is your source of limitless strength.

To think about...

- What feels too hard for you right now?
- How does remembering what the Bible says give you courage?

In Life, Money & Relationships

You Are a Leader – And Leadership Starts with You

"Leadership is not about being in charge. It is about taking care of those in your charge."
– Simon Sinek

When you hear the word *leader*, you might picture someone standing on a stage, giving a big speech, or wearing a badge with an official title. But leadership isn't about titles, stages, or popularity. At its core, leadership is about influence, responsibility, and the impact you make on the people around you. And here's the truth: you are already a leader.

You may not always feel like it, but every day, the way you live your life is influencing someone; whether it's a younger sibling watching how you act, a classmate noticing how you handle challenges, or a friend learning from the way you treat others. Leadership starts with you, right where you are.

Leaders don't wait for permission to make a difference. They step up when it matters. Sometimes leadership looks like speaking out against something unfair or being the one who helps when others walk away. Other times, it looks quieter; like listening to a friend who needs to talk, setting a good example with your work ethic, or simply showing kindness when no one else does. You don't need to be the loudest person in the room to lead. You just need the courage to live in a way that inspires others.

But leadership also comes with responsibility. Great leaders aren't perfect; they're willing to learn and grow. They admit when they're wrong, ask for forgiveness, and work to improve. They treat people with respect, no matter who they are. True leadership isn't about bossing others around, it's about serving others and making them better.

Most importantly, leadership that lasts doesn't come from trying to impress people. It comes from leaning on God for wisdom, strength, and direction. When you put Him first, He shapes your character and helps you lead with confidence and purpose.

So don't underestimate yourself. You don't need to wait until you're older, richer, or more "important" to be a leader. You are a leader now: through your choices, your actions, and your example. Use your influence wisely. Be brave enough to step up, even in small ways. Because every time you choose to do what's right, you're showing others what real leadership looks like.

Wisdom in One Line: You are a leader, right here, right now. And the world needs your light.

To think about...

- Who looks up to you without you even realising it?
- What's one small way you can lead by example this week?

With God as your anchor, you can face anything. Yet life will always bring new challenges, temptations, and opportunities that require daily wisdom. That's why this book closes with bonus treasures—timeless reminders you can carry with you wherever you go. Think of them as keys you'll return to again and again as your journey continues.

Bonus Lessons: Treasures for the Journey

"The beautiful thing about learning is that no one can take it away from you."
– B.B. King

Every book has an ending, but wisdom never does. Life will always stretch beyond the lessons neatly written in chapters, presenting you with fresh challenges, new opportunities, and unexpected turns. That's why this final section isn't just an "extra" add-on; it's a reminder that growth, purpose, and wisdom are lifelong pursuits.

Think of these bonus lessons as treasures you tuck into your pocket for the road ahead. They are not here to overwhelm you with more information but to leave you with guiding truths you can return to when life gets noisy. Research shows that people who regularly reflect on what they've learned are 23% more likely to apply it effectively in real life (*Harvard Business Review, 2014*). Reflection makes knowledge stick, turning words into action.

You'll find in these pages lessons that act like anchors; principles to hold onto when the ground beneath your feet feels shaky. Some are reminders of values that may seem *small*, like gratitude or kindness, but in reality, they carry immense weight. Others push you to think bigger, to dream beyond your current horizon, and to stretch into the person you are becoming.

Consider them like the last pieces of advice a mentor shares before you step out into the world on your own. They don't replace what you've already learned; they reinforce it. They whisper in your ear when you're tempted to forget who you are, or when you need encouragement to take the next brave step.

One of the most powerful things about wisdom is that it multiplies when you use it. The more you apply these truths in your daily life, the more they'll expand; shaping your character, influencing others, and leaving an imprint that outlives you. Legacy isn't built in one grand gesture; it's woven into the everyday choices you make.

So, as you enter this final section, pause for a moment. Think back on everything you've read and learned so far. Which lessons struck a chord? Which ones do you need to revisit? Which ones will you carry forward as non-negotiables in your life?

The journey doesn't end here. It only deepens. These bonus lessons are gifts—simple, timeless, and enduring—because sometimes the smallest keys unlock the greatest doors.

50 Things to Help You Win

In Life, Money & Relationships

What to Do When You're Tempted

How can you stay on the right path and keep your heart pure? By following God's word and staying close to Him with all your heart.

Let's be real, temptation is everywhere. From social media trends to peer pressure, from cheating on a test to telling a *harmless* lie, the struggle is real. The world is full of things pulling us in the wrong direction, and that's not going to change. But here's the good news: God has given us the strength and wisdom to stand strong when temptation comes.

The Bible makes it clear that the way to overcome temptation isn't just by gritting your teeth and relying on willpower. The ancient Scriptures tell us that the key is to *seek God with all your heart* and live according to His word. That means making Him your priority, being honest with Him about your struggles, and leaning on His strength when you feel weak.

Picture this: you forgot to study for a big test, and the person next to you has all the answers in plain sight. The urge to sneak a peek feels strong. It seems small, but in that moment, you're at a crossroads—you can give in, or you can turn to God for help.

The truth is, God isn't standing over you with a hammer, ready to punish you if you slip up. He loves you, and He wants to help you. He wants you to be honest with Him, to admit when you're struggling, and to trust Him for the strength you need.

The more time you spend with God—reading His word, praying, and building your relationship with Him—the stronger you'll be when temptation shows up. You won't be perfect (none of us are), but you'll be better equipped to make the right choice.

Temptation will always come. But with God's help, you don't have to fall for it.

Wisdom in One Line: God's word is your shield in moments of weakness.

To think about...

- What temptation do you face most often?
- How could prayer or Scripture help you stand strong in that moment?

In Life, Money & Relationships

Watch What They Do

You get to know people, not really by what they say, but by what they do.

Words are powerful. They can inspire, comfort, or even cut deeply. Think about the last time someone said something that made you really angry—you probably felt your emotions flare up almost instantly. That's the power of words. But as strong as words are, they are not always the truest measure of a person's character.

People can say all the right things. They can tell stories that make them seem kind, trustworthy, or generous. For example, imagine a friend tells you they once saw a hungry person and were so heartbroken they nearly cried. As they describe how much it bothered them, you may walk away thinking, *Wow, this person must be so compassionate.*

But here's the test: do their actions match their words? Someone who claims to hate seeing people suffer but then turns around and bullies classmates, spreads gossip, or treats others unkindly is showing you something very different. Their words may say one thing, but their actions reveal the truth.

That's why it's so important to pay attention not just to what people *say* but to what they *do*. If you ever feel confused about someone—if their words and behaviour don't quite line up—*turn down the volume* on their words and watch their actions instead. Actions will always tell the real story.

And this applies to you too. If you want to be seen as kind, then show kindness. If you want to be known as honest, then live honestly. It's not enough to say the right things, you have to live them out. Your actions are what people will remember most.

Always remember: a person's actions reveal their character far more clearly than their words ever could. So don't just listen, watch. Don't just talk, do what you say.

Wisdom in One Line: Trust actions more than promises.

To think about...

- Do the actions of your friends line up with their words?
- What do your own actions say about you?

In Life, Money & Relationships

Your Getting Starts from Giving

"No one has ever become poor by giving."
– Anne Frank

Have you ever noticed how everything in life moves in cycles? The sun rises and sets, seasons come around, rain falls to the ground only to rise again as vapour. Even your own body works in rhythms; your heart beats in a steady cycle, blood flows in and out, breath comes and goes. Life itself is built on these rhythms, and one of the most powerful cycles you can choose to participate in is the cycle of giving and receiving.

At first, giving may seem like a loss. You share your time, your energy, or your money, and it feels like something has been taken from you. But in reality, giving is never subtraction; it is multiplication in disguise.

Think about planting a seed. You drop a tiny seed into the soil, and from the outside it looks like you've lost it forever, but with time, care, and patience, that single seed becomes a tree that produces multiples of new seeds.

Giving works the same way. Every time you give—whether it's kindness, encouragement, or help—you're planting seeds that will one day grow into a harvest, often far greater than what you originally gave.

And here's the amazing part: giving doesn't always have to be big to be powerful. A smile to someone who feels invisible might brighten their whole day. A kind word to a classmate could give them the courage to keep going when they're close to giving up. Offering your time to help a friend with homework or your parents with chores might seem small, but those acts of service create ripples that spread further than you realise.

Psychologists even say that people who give regularly experience more happiness, stronger relationships, and better mental health. In other words, giving isn't just good for others, it's good for you too.

The secret is to give freely, without expecting anything in return. That's when the cycle really works. When you give with a generous heart, God finds unexpected ways to give back to you—sometimes through opportunities, friendships, or blessings you couldn't have planned for yourself.

So, don't hold back. Be generous with your words, your time, your talents, and your resources. It's not about how much you have, but about what you do with what you have. When you step into the rhythm of giving, you open yourself up to the rhythm of receiving. That's how life blossoms; in beautiful, surprising, and unforgettable ways.

Wisdom in One Line: The more you give with a generous heart, the more room you create to receive life's greatest blessings.

In Life, Money & Relationships

To think about...

- When was the last time giving made you feel happy inside?
- What's one way you can give today without expecting anything back?

50 Things to Help You Win

In Life, Money & Relationships

The Power of Recognition: Learning to Notice Difference

"When you recognise a moment, you unlock its potential."
– Mike Murdock

One of the most valuable skills you can develop in life is the ability to recognise difference—difference in moments, in people, and even in yourself. This is sometimes called the **Law of Recognition**: the idea that opportunities, wisdom, and growth are already around you, but you can only benefit from them if you learn to recognise them.

1. Recognise the Difference in Moments

Not every moment in your life is the same. Some are routine, like brushing your teeth or catching the bus, while others carry the potential to change your future. Maybe it's the moment to apologise and restore a broken friendship, or the courage to raise your hand in class when you usually stay quiet. It might not look significant at first, but recognising the uniqueness of that moment could shift the direction of your life.

In the story of David in the Bible, while everyone else only saw a terrifying giant, David recognised something different; an opportunity to trust God and step into his destiny. That single moment of recognition set the stage for his future as a king.

2. Recognise the Difference in People

Every person you meet carries something unique: a gift, an insight, or an experience that you could learn from. A teacher may seem strict, but behind that firmness might be wisdom that could guide your life beyond the classroom. A friend's quirky talent could be the very thing that inspires you to grow in your own area.

Noticing the difference in people also builds respect. When you acknowledge someone's unique strengths, you affirm their value. It's like saying, *"I see you, and what you bring to the table matters."* That recognition often opens doors to friendships, mentorships, and opportunities you might otherwise have missed.

3. Recognise the Difference in Yourself

This might be the hardest part. It's often easier to see what others are good at than to notice your own gifts. But recognising your uniqueness is essential to discovering your purpose. Maybe you're the one who always encourages others, or perhaps you're skilled at problem-solving, creativity, or simply listening well. These are not random traits, they are God-given abilities purposed by God to bless the world.

A Story to Remember

Amarjit was shy and often felt invisible. When her teacher asked for volunteers to plan the school's cultural day, she almost stayed quiet. But something inside told her this was her moment. She raised her hand.

Through the process, Amarjit discovered she was gifted at organising tasks and keeping the team on track. Her teacher noticed too and praised her for her exemplary leadership qualities. By recognising that moment, the encouragement of her teacher, and her own hidden strength, Amarjit stepped into opportunities she never thought possible including later becoming head of her school's events committee.

Why This Matters

Opportunities don't always come wrapped in neon signs. They hide in conversations, in subtle body language, in the people you meet, and in the quiet nudges of your own gifts. If you're not paying attention, you might miss them. Learning to notice the difference sharpens your awareness and helps you unlock treasures that can shape your destiny.

Wisdom in One Line: When you learn to recognise the difference in moments, people, and yourself, you open the door to opportunities that can change your life.

To think about...

- What's one *moment* you might be overlooking right now?
- Who in your life carries wisdom you could learn from if you paid attention?

In Life, Money & Relationships

Respect Time: Use It Wisely

"Lost time is never found again."
– Benjamin Franklin

Time is one of the most precious gifts you'll ever receive, yet it's the one thing many people treat carelessly. You can earn more money, buy new clothes, or even make new friends but once a moment is gone, you may never get it back. That's why it's so important to respect time and use it wisely.

Think about it: each day, every single person on Earth gets the exact same 24 hours. No one gets extra, not even billionaires or world leaders. The difference isn't in the amount of time we're given, but in how we choose to use it. Studies show that people who plan and use their time intentionally are not only more productive but also experience less stress and greater satisfaction in life.

Respecting time doesn't mean cramming every second with work or study. It means recognising that time is valuable and choosing how to spend it with purpose. Scrolling endlessly on social media or binge-watching shows might feel fun in the moment, but hours slip away that could have been used to build your future, strengthen your relationships, or simply rest well.

When you respect time, you treat it like a resource you don't want to waste. That means you:

- **Prioritise what matters.** Do the important things first: schoolwork, family, your relationship with God, before distractions steal your focus.
- **Guard against procrastination.** Putting things off feels easier, but it often creates more stress later.
- **Make room for balance.** Time for fun, creativity, and rest is just as important as study or work. Wise use of time is about balance, not burnout.

The Bible puts it this way: *"Teach us to number our days, that we may gain a heart of wisdom"* (Psalm 90:12). When you realise your time is limited, you begin to use it with wisdom.

Remember, how you use your time today is shaping who you'll become tomorrow. So, respect it. Treasure it. Don't let it slip away unnoticed. Instead, spend it in ways that build you up, bless others, and brings you closer to the life God has planned for you.

Wisdom in One Line: Respect time by using it wisely because every moment wasted is a moment you can never get back.

To think about...

- What's your biggest timewaster right now?
- How could you use your time better this week?

Conclusion

A Final Word of Blessing

As you come to the end of this book, remember that wisdom is not something you finish reading—it's something you start living. Each lesson in these pages is a seed. When planted in your heart and watered with practice, it will grow.

You don't have to live all fifty lessons perfectly. Just begin with one thought, one choice, one act of courage at a time. Be patient with yourself. Growth takes time, and even small steps forward still move you in the right direction.

Carry these truths with you as companions through every stage of your life. When you're unsure, return to them. When you're afraid, lean on them. When you're tempted to give up, let them remind you that you were made for more.

May your heart always be open to learning, your hands ready to serve, your mind anchored in truth, and your spirit full of light.

May you walk boldly in your uniqueness, handle money wisely, build lasting relationships, and live with excellence and integrity.

May you remember that you are deeply loved, endlessly capable, and never alone.

And above all, may your life reflect God's wisdom, kindness, and grace—shining brightly for all to see.

If you learnt anything at all from this book, remember to pass it on to a friend. It could contain the answers they need to some of life's perplexing questions.

In Life, Money & Relationships

50 Things to Help You Win

www.ingramcontent.com/pod-product-compliance
Lightning Source LLC
Chambersburg PA
CBHW020838160426
43192CB00007B/707